Moments for HOME SCHOOL Moms

52 Weekly Devotionals

BETH SHARPTON

Moments for HOME SCHOOL Moms

52 Weekly Devotionals

published by
🌐 **AMG** *Publishers*

Moments for Homeschool Moms

Copyright © 2003 by Beth Sharpton
Published by AMG Publishers
6815 Shallowford Rd.
Chattanooga, Tennessee 37421

Unless otherwise indicated, all Scripture quotations are taken from the HOLY BIBLE, NEW INTERNATIONAL VERSION® NIV®. Copyright ©1973, 1978, 1984 by International Bible Society. Used by permission of Zondervan Publishing House. All rights reserved.

Scripture quotations marked (NLT) are taken from the *Holy Bible, New Living Translation,* copyright © 1996. Used by permission of Tyndale House Publishers, Inc., Wheaton, Illinois 60189. All rights reserved.

Scripture quotations market (TLB) are taken from *The Living Bible* © 1971 owned by assignment by Illiniois Regional Bank N. A. (as trustee), used by permission of Tyndale House Publishers, Inc., Wheaton, Illinois 60189. All rights reserved.

Scripture quotations marked (*The Message*) are taken from *THE MESSAGE,* Copyright © 1993, 1994, 1995, 1996, 2000, 2001, 2002. Used by permission of NavPress Publishing Group. All rights reserved.

ISBN 0-89957-364-9

First printing—June 2003

Cover designed by ImageWright, Inc., Chattanooga, Tennessee
Interior design and typesetting by Reider Publishing Services,
     West Hollywood, California
Edited and proofread by g. Susan Wilt, Robert Kelly, Jody El-Assadi,
     Dan Penwell, and Judy Gordon Morrow

Printed in Canada
09 08 07 06 05 04 03 – T – 8 7 6 5 4 3 2 1

I dedicate this book to
my mentors-encouragers,
my mom Joanne Aebischer
and Jerrie Hosford.
Your praise and loving critique
motivated me to be the
best writer I can be for the Lord.
Your help has been invaluable to me.

Acknowledgment

Thanks to my husband, Jeff, whose unconditional love and prayers have provided me with great strength of purpose in my roles as a home-schooling mom, writer, and woman of God.

And to Kathy Dole and Linda Baker—you're the best friends and sisters anyone ever had. Thank you for your counsel, prayer, and praise.

And to my girls, Tara and Launa—I'm so glad God has blessed our home with your love and laughter.

And to Dan, my editor. Thank you for your hard work and for your friendship.

Contents

CONTENTS

November: Serving

December: Stewardship

January: My God Carries Me

February: Distractions

CONTENTS

March: Blessings

April: Discipline

May: God's Will

June: Making the Grade

CONTENTS

July: Growing

August: Bearing Fruit

Foreword

The theme of this book is best introduced in dramatic fashion. Sit back, relax, and enjoy the show!

Cast: Benny—a man pulling his god in a wagon

Idol—a man playing the part of Benny's god, or a large stuffed animal

God—a man playing the part of God

Doug—a man being carried by his God

(Benny enters stage right, pulling a wagon with a large idol in it. From the opposite direction comes God carrying Doug. They meet center stage.)

Doug (speaking to Benny): What have you got in the wagon? It looks heavy!

Benny (wiping his forehead): It is! (He gestures proudly.) This is my god.

Doug (looking at the god unimpressed): Hmmm . . . I see. Well, what does your god do?

Benny: Do? Oh . . . (works hard to get his god into an upright position, then turns to Doug with enthusiasm) There he is!

Doug: Yes, I see him, but what does he do?

Benny: Well, I take him with me wherever I go—he's my god, you know. I keep him dusted, so he's always shiny and beautiful. I bring him offerings of food and fine clothing, and then, I bow down before him in worship.
(For the first time, Benny notices Doug is not standing.) Hey, what have you got there?

Doug (looking satisfied): This is my God!
(Benny appears impressed. He walks around Doug's God, inspecting him.)

Benny: Yeah, he looks okay. So, what does your God do?

Doug: Wow, too many things to count! My God gives me food and rest, he guides me and comforts me, and best of all, he loves me—just because I'm me!

Benny (leans forward, obviously interested): Really!

Doug: Yes, *my* God carries *me*. (God, carrying Doug, exits stage right as Benny can only watch, dumbfounded.)
(Benny, then exits stage left, now looking at his god with increasing irritation. He's beginning to think his god is more trouble than he's worth.)

1 *Sept.*

"I'm Afeared!"

"Be strong and courageous. Do not be afraid or discouraged because of the king of Assyria and the vast army with him, for there is a greater power with us than with him. With him is only the arm of flesh, but with us is the LORD our God to help us and to fight our battles." And the people gained confidence from what Hezekiah the king of Judah said. (2 Chron. 32:7, 8)

In the movie, *The Little Kidnappers,* two brothers, eight-year-old Harry and five-year-old Davy, are preparing to sail from their Scottish homeland to Canada. They are going to live with their grandparents after the deaths of their mother and father. When they arrive, it doesn't take them long to figure out that their grandfather has been harboring a long-standing grudge against their now deceased father. He dismisses their boyish exuberance and rejects their attempts to love him. Although Harry and David do not understand the reason for their grandfather's bitterness, they suffer from its effects daily.[1]

The story continues when the boys find a baby abandoned on the sandy beach near their new home. Knowing how their grandfather would react, they decide to keep their discovery a secret and take care of the baby themselves. Grandfather has already denied them a puppy, so Harry and David are not about to share this secret with him, or anyone else.

However, after babysitting for two days, the boys find they are in way over their heads. The poor baby will not stop crying. He's cold and hungry in their makeshift hideout of driftwood, and neither of the boys knows how to help him. They take turns watching the baby day and night, but what begins as an innocent substitution for love quickly turns into an impossible burden for them to bear. When Grandfather locks Harry in the woodshed for venturing onto a forbidden hill, the real nightmare begins in earnest. David is now alone to care for the baby, and a fierce storm is rapidly approaching.

Panicking, David rushes to the shed and tries desperately to free his brother. It's hopeless. The lock won't budge. Anxiously, he decides to return to the hideout, but just as he starts off, a deafening crack of thunder and a blinding flash of lightning send him scrambling back to the safety of the locked shed.

"I'm afeared! I'm afeared!" he yells into the storm.

Thunder booms again, and David jumps with fright. Another streak of lightning fills the night sky, illuminating it with an eerie glow. David turns and sees what he thinks is a monstrous giant, unaware that it is only a pair of Grandfather's long underwear flapping in the wind. He stands rooted to the spot in terror.

Recovering somewhat, David bolts away from the apparition screaming, "I'm afeared! I'm afeared!"

The driving rain propels him toward the house and smack into the one thing he fears even more than the storm— his grandfather. Needless to say, David can't see how things can get any worse. But, unbeknownst to David, this is exactly what he needed.

The entire village has been searching for the lost baby, assuming he's been kidnapped. Grandfather is the only person who can explain what's happened and appease the town's anger over the mess David and Harry have created.

In spite of his harsh exterior, Grandfather intervenes on their behalf and the boys realize he truly does love them.

Often, I am like young David, running to and fro in the fierce storm of my circumstances, crying, "I'm afeared! I'm afeared!" All the while, the One I need is waiting to help me. Unlike David and Harry's grandfather, God is not gruff, nor does he hold grudges or stifle me with rules that have no purpose. Even in the midst of my own fearful storm, he calls me to turn to him for comfort.

Are there times when you're running away from God?

Rather than running away, as David did, run toward God. It matters little whether you're a new homeschool teacher or have been teaching for years. Perhaps you're battling a willful, disobedient child, tackling never-ending chores, or facing unwanted advice from well-meaning family and friends. Whatever you're running from, God says to you, as he did to Hezekiah, "Be strong and courageous. Do not be afraid or discouraged."

God himself will be your refuge on those days when you feel like a prime target for the enemy. You don't need ever be "afeared" again. His presence, power, and peace are yours.

Dear Lord, thank you for being my loving heavenly Father. I know I can run to you with any problem, yet I often bolt at the first sign of danger. Thank you for calming my fears. Thank you for fighting my battles. And, most of all, thank you for being the Teacher in my home. Help me remember I don't have to do this alone. Amen.

2

Let God Provide the Light

Who among you fears the LORD and obeys the word of his servant? Let him who walks in the dark, who has no light, trust in the name of the LORD and rely on his God. But now, all you who light fires and provide yourselves with flaming torches, go, walk in the light of your fires and the torches you have set ablaze. (Isa. 50:10, 11)

I was attending a women's retreat with my Sunday school class, and our meeting had just broken up. I headed out into the night, armed with my trusty flashlight. It was a quiet, lovely evening with majestic ponderosa pines towering above me. Twinkling stars were peeping through the velvety black sky. Just then, a group of women drove up and asked if I wanted a lift back to our cabin.

"Oh, I'm fine, thanks. I'll enjoy the walk," I said. "I'll see you back there in a little while."

The cabin was about a half-mile from the main meeting-house, and I'd planned earlier to walk back after the evening session. I was looking forward to the fresh air and exercise. They waved and drove on.

As soon as the car rounded the bend my flashlight began to flicker. I began walking much faster, but soon realized the battery was failing. It wouldn't be long before I'd be completely engulfed in darkness. Seconds later, that's exactly what happened. I was alone in the inky blackness, and there were no other lights for miles around. I'd never been in such utter darkness. Even in my neighborhood at night, there's always a streetlight or a neighbor's porch light to help me find my way. But out here there was nothing. I began walking slowly, praying fervently for God to help me find the cabin.

It wasn't long (although it seemed like forever) before I saw a light flickering in the distance. "Thank you, Lord!" leaped from my lips. I quickened my step, careful to avoid objects, such as trees and rocks that might trip me up and send me sprawling on the ground. I strained to keep that light in sight and breathed a sigh of relief when I saw the silhouette of my own car parked near the cabin. The following evening I gladly accepted a ride back after our meeting.

How many times have I refused God in much the same way I refused that ride back to the cabin? He offers to give me a lift and guide me with his perfect light. And instead of acknowledging his provision with gratitude, my response is, "No thanks, God. I've got my own light." How he must shake his head at my foolishness, knowing it won't be long until I call for help. My feeble attempts to make my own way without him always lead me astray.

As home educators, it's possible for us to get lost when we tread the forest of decisions that face us daily: which curriculum to use . . . which extra activities to participate in . . . and which ministries to become involved with. Many times we make these choices without asking God for his input. However, the Bible tells us God longs to light our way, and his radiant light will never fail for lack of a charged battery. His light will never fade or fizzle out.

God is not a dictator; he'll let us try finding our way without him. We can stubbornly squint into the darkness, attempting to see by the flashlight of our own wisdom, or we can let God shine his real light into our lives.

Holy Father, forgive me for trying to light my own way. I know in my heart I can never get anywhere without your guidance, but sometimes I plunge ahead without thinking. I come to you in the darkness, ready to follow your lead. Light my way, Lord. I will trust in you. Amen.

3

Laughing at God

Then the LORD said to Abraham, "Why did Sarah laugh and say, 'Will I really have a child, now that I am old?' Is anything too hard for the LORD?" (Gen. 18:13, 14)

"I'm too old to have a baby!" Sarah laughed with scorn. She lacked faith that God could, or would, keep his word. She didn't believe God was going to create life in her postmenopausal body. After all, she was ninety years old! Imagine having your first baby at the age of ninety. It was truly impossible!

Impossible! That's how I felt when our oldest daughter, Tara, asked me to homeschool her. She'd been doing well in public school for two

8

years. In the fall, Tara would be in second grade and her younger sister, Launa, would be in preschool. With Launa in preschool, I would have two glorious hours every morning to myself. The following year Launa would be in kindergarten, and the year after that I'd have the whole day to myself while they were at school!

Me, homeschool? You've got to be kidding! I thought. *Oh, honey, you don't want me to do that.*

Soon summer was in full swing. I hoped that would be the end of the crazy homeschooling idea, but Tara kept asking. Then came the "knife in the gut" comment that compelled me to ask God what he thought.

"Mommy, I want to be able to pray and talk about Jesus every day," Tara said. "We can't do that in public school."

Private school wasn't even an option. Inwardly I groaned, *Lord, I've never been good with kids. You know how impatient and controlling I am. Anyway, you called me to be a writer. How can I be a writer if I'm stuck teaching kids all day long?*

But, at that moment the Holy Spirit nudged me. "Do you doubt I can work through you, if this is my will?"

No, of course I don't doubt you, Lord! I defended. *But . . . you wouldn't ask this of me, would you?*

It didn't sound like a reasonable option, but I prayed about it, afraid to hear the answer, yet truly wanting God to speak to me. I talked with some area homeschool teachers and before long, I began to see the possibilities. I'd always loved school. Being a homeschooling mom would give me an excuse to buy lots of great books and learn right along with my girls.

Two months later we decided to homeschool the girls. I was excited but still determined to continue my writing career. I was a lot like Sarah. She tried to obtain the child of promise through her own efforts; I tried to be a writer the same way. I was accustomed to writing five days a week, so I kept trying to work the same schedule. But after a full day of school there was housework to do and dinner to cook. The more I forced myself to "do it all," the more miserable life became for all of us.

Weary and discouraged, I placed my writing career at God's feet. *If you want it,* I said silently, *it's yours. I'll only write if you give it back to me.*

Then I began pouring myself fully into homeschooling. That was when my laughter changed from an expression of disbelief to joy. Finally, there was peace in my heart and in our home. Months later, when the days were running smoothly, I felt released to pursue writing again. Somehow, it worked this time.

I'm learning what Sarah learned. Although it's human to laugh at an impossible calling from God, it also shows a weak understanding of his power. My doubts stemmed from insecurity and pride.

Sarah's disbelief mocked the sovereignty of God. No wonder she received such a stern rebuke, but apparently she learned to trust God for the impossible. In 1 Peter 3, she's praised for her obedient and submissive spirit. Looking with wonder at the miracle son in her arms she named him Isaac, meaning *laughter,* saying, "God has brought me laughter, and everyone who hears about this will laugh with me" (Gen. 21:6).

Like Sarah, I look at my children with delight and laugh. Who would have believed that God could possibly make a homeschooling mom out of me?

Oh, Lord, help me see that when I laugh in disbelief, I sin against the One I most want to please. You know me. I don't mean to doubt. I want to believe, but your ways sometimes seem impossible. I guess that's why it takes faith to follow you. Grant me faith, dear Jesus, and take me by the hand. I fear the unknown, but even more, I fear going a step in any direction without you. May my laughter be in harmony with yours, never in discord. Amen.

4

Sustenance in Drought

For this is what the LORD, the God of Israel, says,
"The jar of flour will not be used up and the jug of oil
will not run dry until the day the LORD gives rain on
the land." (1 Kings 17:14)

Elijah probably lost count of how many weeks
he'd been beside the brook in the Kerith
ravine. How long had it been since God had
sent him to tell Ahab there would be no rain
until he gave the word? After delivering this
message to the wicked king and the people of
Israel, Elijah could do nothing else but follow

God's command to take refuge near the brook and wait for further instructions.

His only companions were the ravens. God sent them every morning and evening with food to sustain him. Every day, Elijah awoke to the sound of trickling water from the brook and the fluttering of ravens' wings above his head. Other than those few sounds, he was alone with only the sun, the sky, and his own thoughts to keep him company.

Certainly, Elijah grew weary of his isolation and loneliness. He hated to be ungrateful, but why was he stuck out here in the middle of nowhere? Yes, God was present with him. Yes, he treasured his time with the Lord. But Elijah probably wanted to be with his people, the Jews, even if it meant suffering through the drought with them. Why must he stay out here all alone?

Some time later, the brook that had sustained Elijah all those many weeks dried up. God could have kept the water flowing and continued sending care packages via the ravens, but he chose instead to send Elijah to Zarephath of Sidon. He told Elijah to look for a widow and her son there, saying, "I have commanded a widow in that place to supply you with food" (1 Kings 17:9).

When Elijah found the widow, she was gathering sticks to prepare a last meal for herself and her son. Elijah asked her for water and bread, but the widow told him she had only a handful of flour and a little oil. When Elijah heard this, he told the widow to go ahead and prepare a small cake for him, and then make something for herself and her son. Elijah assured the widow that God would provide for all of them until the rain fell and the crops grew again.

For three years this unlikely trio lived together, ate together, and waited for the rain to come again. They were faithful companions in a land of misery. During this time, the widow's son became ill and died, but God kept his promise to see them through. When Elijah asked God to return the boy's life to his body, God heard him and the boy came back to life.

After a long time, God sent the long-promised rain.

If you feel stranded at the brook, totally out of resources as a homeschooling mom, don't jump to the conclusion that God has stopped providing for you. During these tough times, just as God provided food for Elijah, God's Word should be the food that sustains you. He knows that your time in the desert is the means for producing the faith you need to impact others.

God also knows you need companionship during these times of drought. By joining a homeschooling support group, being active in an evangelical church, and by investing in close friendships with other believers, they can be the means of over-flowing sustenance for your life.

Give God the time he needs, and he will eventually turn your dry resources into a gushing brook.

Dear Lord, I long for your touch in my life, for sustenance to keep me going day by day. It's not easy being a homeschool mom. I know you long to rain your blessings and Spirit on my home. I pray that you'll continue to pour your blessings on my life, my home, and my country. Fill us with your Spirit to do your will. Amen.

Oct.

5

Dressing for the Wedding

"But when the king came in to see the guests, he noticed a man there who was not wearing wedding clothes. 'Friend,' he asked, 'how did you get in here without wedding clothes?' The man was speechless." (Matt. 22:11, 12)

Imagine the mayor of a city walking into a downtown mission and making this declaration to all the homeless people: "My son is getting married and I'm throwing a big party. I'd like all of you to come." But his announcement doesn't end there.

"I've already sent special engraved invitations to my friends and to most of the elite in the city," he continues, "but everyone has refused. Some said they had business meetings, others had golf outings and tennis matches. One man even said he needed to stay home and wash his car that day."

The people in the mission laughed at the crazy reactions of the privileged class.

"As if that weren't bad enough, some of them tore up the invitations and threw them back in my face, and a few of the delivery people were beaten as they tried to deliver the invitations. Worst of all, one group of so-called friends showed up at my house, dragged my son out of his bed, and beat him unconscious."

The crowd grew quiet with shock. Many of them expressed sympathy and concern.

"Oh, he's fine now, but those thugs will certainly get what's coming to them." The group murmured in agreement.

"Anyway, the caterer has prepared a huge banquet, the band's been hired, and I hate to have everything go to waste. Won't all of you come and celebrate with me?"

"And don't worry about your clothes. I've bought new outfits for everyone. All of you are going to be sharply dressed for this wedding. This is a big occasion."

Most of these destitute people agree this is an offer too good to refuse. They quickly shower, dress in their fancy new clothes, and eagerly pile into the limousines waiting outside the door. But some hang back, unconvinced of the mayor's offer and ashamed of their filthy, ragged appearance. The mayor immediately notices their concern and assures them there are enough new clothes for them too. Relieved, they hurry off to get ready and join the others already headed to the mayor's home.

A short time later, as the mayor waits for everyone to arrive for the wedding feast, he notices one man who obviously hasn't cleaned up and is still wearing the same smelly clothes he had on at the mission.

"Why didn't you shower and change into the new clothes I brought along for you?" the mayor asks. "The wedding is about to begin and you're not even ready."

"Well, I think my own clothes look pretty good," replies the man. "You wouldn't turn me away just because I'm dirty and not all duded up in new threads, would you?"

Furious, the mayor throws him out.

When Jesus told a similar parable of the wedding banquet, his listeners understood the meaning. All have been invited and all can attend, but those who refuse this free offer (and the free garments) will suffer eternal banishment from the Lord.

The single most important lesson we can teach our children is that even though we dress ourselves up in good works, impeccable manners, high achievement, and community service, none of the clothes in our closet will make an impression on God. Only the new clothes provided by God and bought with the blood of Jesus are acceptable.

Jesus told lots of stories and used plenty of examples from everyday life to teach important truths. As homeschool moms, we must do the same.

O God, my King, help me teach my children the importance of God's grace. I need to be reminded of it often. Any pride I feel in my wardrobe is quickly forgotten whenever I get a glimpse of Christ's radiant garments. Forgive me, Lord. I ask that your holiness replace my filthy rags of pride and self-righteousness. Amen.

6

Whitewashed Tombs

"Woe to you teachers of the law and Pharisees, you hypocrites! You are like whitewashed tombs, which look beautiful on the outside but on the inside are full of dead men's bones and everything unclean. In the same way, on the outside you appear to people as righteous but on the inside you are full of hypocrisy and wickedness." (Matt. 23:27, 28)

"I want to keep my room neat and clean," my daughter, Tara, said to me one day. "Come take a look."

"Yes, it looks beautiful," I replied.

And yet I couldn't resist a peek inside her closet. Opening the door, I discovered a stack of clothes, shoes, toys, and other assorted treasures three feet high. I grinned and gave her *the mom look.*

"Your room looks wonderful as long as you don't open the closet doors," I said, "but it's not really clean, is it? It's like a whitewashed tomb."

"What do you mean?" Tara asked. "What's a whitewashed tomb?"

"Remember when Jesus called the Pharisees hypocrites because they pretended to be something they weren't? These Pharisees followed the rules, went to all the religious services, and outwardly did all the right things. Their lives reminded Jesus of fancy tombs, all clean and whitewashed, but rotten inside. The inside of even a nice white tomb is still full of dead people's bones."

"Maybe I ought to clean out my closet," Tara admitted.

"Good idea," I agreed.

A few days later I went to the grocery store after a particularly difficult school day. I'd lost my temper several times and pushed the girls through their subjects just to get them done. I'd tried to cram too many things into one day and felt guilty about my poor planning and ugly attitude. I was grateful to get away from my girls for a while to regroup. As Patsy Clairmont would say, I was "sportin' a 'tude!"

My friend Kelly was at the cash register as I prepared to check out. Her smile warmed me. After the usual hellos, she gushed, "You're such a great mom! You teach your girls at home and do so many fun things with them, and you're an author, too. You're just so good!"

I told her I'm just a normal mom who makes a lot of mistakes, but she was determined to place me firmly on the pedestal of perfection. Kelly was painting me with whitewash but I knew what was really inside of me—ugly things she couldn't see.

What Kelly couldn't see, Jesus could. He knows of the rotten attitudes and unspiritual thinking in my heart and life. Every day I ask him to clear away my sinful attitudes and critical thoughts. I must constantly look to him for guidance in correct decisions for my family, my life, and my teaching.

The Pharisees had an air of holiness, but it was all camouflage. God knew their hearts. I don't want to make that same mistake. I don't want any camouflage in my life. I do want to be holy, but I can't do it alone. Only because the Spirit of God lives inside me can I even think about coming close to the perfection God wants. I certainly know it's not enough just to look the part.

Dear Lord, sometimes people think because we homeschool our children we are extra religious. It's only that we've felt your call to teach our children at home. It can be a difficult calling at times, but no more devout or difficult than the work you've given others to do: missionaries, youth leaders, public school teachers, or homemakers. Cleanse me from the inside out, Lord. Keep me from self-pride, as well as dejection. And whatever gleam of purity might emanate from my life, I'll give you the glory for it. Amen.

7

Germ Warfare

The Pharisees and some of the teachers of the law who had come from Jerusalem gathered around Jesus and saw some of his disciples eating food with hands that were "unclean," that is, unwashed. (The Pharisees and all the Jews do not eat unless they give their hands a ceremonial washing, holding to the tradition of the elders. . . .)

So the Pharisees and teachers of the law asked Jesus, "Why don't your disciples live according to the tradition of the elders instead of eating their food with 'unclean' hands?"

He replied, "Isaiah was right when he prophesied about you hypocrites; as it is written: "'These people honor me with their lips, but their hearts are far from me. They worship me in vain; their teachings are but rules taught by men.' You have let go of the commands of God and are holding on to the traditions of men." (Mark 7:1–8)

My sister Kathy could not get her three-year-old daughter Amy to wash her hands regularly until the child learned about germs.

"Now we have a clean freak in the house," Kathy said with a laugh. "Amy walks out of the bathroom with her hands clean and scrubbed, holding them up as if she's a doctor preparing for surgery. She's afraid to touch anything because she might get GERMS on them."

I can picture the Pharisees complaining to Jesus about the dirty hands of his disciples: "Just who do these guys think they are anyway, flaunting our traditions?"

"They're unclean!"

"These fellows are going to defile all of us with their dirty hands!"

Jesus wasn't opposed to cleanliness. He hated hypocrisy— ritual masquerading as righteousness. The Pharisees' worshiped in vain because they were hoping to find acceptance by keeping the Law.

Jesus came to release us from this burden. He condensed the teaching of the Law into just two commands when he said, " 'Love the Lord your God with all your heart and with all your soul and with all your mind' . . . and the second is like it: 'Love your neighbor as yourself' " (Matt. 22:37–39).

Truthfully, I could work on those two commands for a long time and never need another list, but it sounded too easy to the Pharisees. They stretched the Law into hundreds of detailed rules that told the people what to do, when and where to do it, and how often. They appeared righteous in their traditions, all the while retaining greed, pride, and malice within their hearts. Touting man-made rules, they walked proudly and rolled their eyes at anyone who couldn't or wouldn't keep them to the letter.

I grew up in a Christian family that attended every church service. We dressed up for worship, sang the old hymns, read the Bible regularly, and prayed together. Those were all good things, but none of them can earn God's acceptance. God's grace is a gift. I want my children to understand that we perform so-called religious duties out of love toward a gracious God—and not because we're trying to earn his acceptance.

As homeschool moms, we probably teach some rules as spiritual necessities when, in fact, they are only the traditions of human beings—not God. Perhaps our children will question them; I hope they do. The point of educating them at home is not so they can learn a list of religious rules, but to ground them in spiritual truths and show them how to use these truths in every aspect of their lives.

Jesus' warning applies to us all: "You have let go of the commands of God and are holding on to the traditions of men." My deepest desire is to hold onto his commands—loving, honoring, and worshiping him, and loving my neighbor as myself. I must release my grip on meaningless rituals that distract from the heart of worship and holy living.

Dear Father, you know how I love tradition. I'm comfortable with stained glass, padded pews, one-hour services, and low-key worship. I like unmarked, unpierced bodies, and real fingernails. I'm apt to cling to the ways of my upbringing as the only correct way to be a Christian and to judge others who don't follow my rules. Help me see the spirit of your Word and practice true holiness that brings honor to you. Grant me eyes to recognize you, even in an unfamiliar package. Amen.

8

Taking Notes

When they saw the courage of Peter and John and realized that they were unschooled, ordinary men, they were astonished and they took note that these men had been with Jesus. (Acts 4:13)

Gladys Aylward, after learning of the desperate spiritual needs of the Chinese people, felt the call to be a missionary in China. Excited to begin a lifelong, godly adventure, she became a student at the China Inland Mission in London. For three years she diligently studied to learn the language, but was ultimately rejected by the missionary society.

"You're not qualified," the mission president said. "I'm sure you are willing, Miss Aylward. It's just that by the time you reach the level of competence we desire for our missionaries you will be almost thirty years old. Everyone here agrees it is nearly impossible to learn the Chinese language at that advanced age." [2]

This didn't stop Gladys. With God's help she made it to China in 1930. Leaving England with no financial support and less than ten dollars of her own money, she eventually arrived at the inland city of Yangchen. She didn't know the language and lacked a proper education, but God used her anyway.

For many years, this former London parlor maid ran an inn where Chinese merchants stopped each night to rest and refresh themselves and their mule caravans. Every evening she served the drivers steaming bowls of rice right along with Bible stories. They, in turn, spread the stories all across China as they traveled selling their wares. And through Gladys's witness, a Mandarin (a public official of the Chinese Empire) in her district was converted to Christianity.

By order of this same Mandarin, Gladys served as the chief foot inspector for the district. Equipped with his authority and soldiers, Gladys effectively wiped out foot binding, a custom that had painfully crippled women in China for centuries. This humble act of service created yet another way for Gladys to spread the gospel.

When World War II broke out, scores of Chinese children were left without parents or homes, so they were brought to Gladys for shelter and safekeeping. Eventually conditions worsened in Yangchen, and Gladys was forced to flee to the government orphanage at Sian, taking with her over 100 orphans entrusted to her care. They struggled over the mountains on foot, dodging gunfire and fighting starvation. Miraculously, they safely crossed the river just as enemy troops swarmed over the area.

The secret to Gladys's success was the same as that of Peter and John. She had spent time with Jesus and was empowered by the Holy Spirit. The world took note of her courage, just as the Sanhedrin took note of Peter's and John's. That was the only qualification God required of them.

Do you feel like an ordinary woman? Perhaps you didn't graduate from college, and don't hold a teaching degree. There are probably days when you don't feel qualified to be the sole educator of your children. Many homeschooling moms can be daunted by all the requirements:

Professor of all subjects
Scheduling dynamo
Cab driver
Disciplinarian
And, above all, a model of faith.

Peter and John had been fishermen all their lives. They had no training in public speaking, no medical or evangelistic training, and yet they confounded the Sanhedrin by healing the sick and turned their world upside down.

Gladys Aylward's work as a parlor maid doesn't seem like the most effective preparation for winning the masses in China either. But like Peter and John she was discipled and empowered by the same Teacher.

As homeschool moms, we may be intimidated by math problems we've never seen before. When people ask us how we plan to teach our children topics we never studied when we were in school, we can answer boldly, "I'll do my part to research and study, using all the resources available to me, and Jesus will bless my efforts."

Help for academic questions are available in teachers' manuals or from friends. But for the *big* answers to life and faith that stump us, we know the One who has all the answers and he will give us wisdom.

Let's accept our calling with such courage that others will take note that we've been with Jesus. Gladys Aylward praised God that, "one so insignificant, uneducated, and ordinary in every way could be used to his glory for the blessing of his people."[3]

May the same be said of us.

Dear Lord, I feel unprepared to do this job. I don't remember learning much in history. I'm just beginning to understand English diagramming.

And math—well, you gave me very understanding teachers. And now that I'm responsible for the education of others, I need you to guide me as I study and prepare lessons. Help me to focus on the most important part of their education—that they might know you, love you, and serve you all their lives. Please give this ordinary woman your extraordinary wisdom. Amen.

9

What's Your Face Saying?

The look on their faces testifies against them. (Isa. 3:9)

"Are you mad at me?" five-year-old Tara asked.

"No, what makes you say that?" I said.

"Because you have on your *mad face*."

That surprised me. I didn't know I had a *mad face*. Actually, I was fine, concentrating, yes, but certainly not angry. Her question made me wonder what my face said to the world every day. If my own daughter thinks I'm angry, then those who don't know me as well might also have the same impression.

Lloyd Ogilvie says, in *God's Best for My Life*:

What is on our faces, not our words, is the medium of our message. Often our faces deny our faith. Our faces may be an introduction for others to Christ or a negation of what he could mean in their lives. Who would want to know Christ personally because of what is on your face? How should our faces look because we have talked to God?[4]

I want my day-to-day countenance to reflect what I'm teaching my children about Christianity. Do I look like a happy, fulfilled person of faith? If not, perhaps I need to change my facial expression, reminding myself that Jesus has forgiven my sins and now I'm free! That's enough to make anyone put on a happy face.

Moses' face radiated the glory of God after he spent time with him, but that glory faded. It doesn't have to be that way for us. After Jesus rose from the dead, he sent his Spirit to dwell within us. Our faces can be radiant all the time! I can exit my prayer closet glowing from God's presence and keep shining all day long, if I don't allow my circumstances to cancel out his glory.

If actions speak louder than words, then faces must be equally eloquent. I've heard that our facial wrinkles reveal our lifetime habits, whether etching anger and worry on our brow, or revealing evidence of frequent laughter. So, I'd better wipe off that *mad face* and put on a *saved by Jesus* face instead. Then it won't matter how many wrinkles I have 'cause they'll all be in the right places!

What do others see when they look at you? Do they see Christ? Do they see peace, joy, and contentment? Or does your face testify otherwise?

Sweet Jesus, remind me to smile more often and allow my face to reflect your glory—even when I'm tired and stressed out. Give me a hopeful expression, not an artificial mask. Allow my face to always testify that I know you and I love you. Let your light shine in me, Lord. Amen.

10

Who Are the Least?

"Then the righteous will answer him, 'Lord, when did we see you hungry and feed you, or thirsty and give you something to drink? When did we see you a stranger and invite you in, or needing clothes and clothe you? When did we see you sick or in prison and go to visit you?'

"The King will reply, 'I tell you the truth, whatever you did for one of the least of these brothers of mine, you did for me.' . . .

"Then he will say to those on his left . . . "They also will answer, 'Lord, when did we see you hungry or thirsty or a stranger or needing clothes or sick or in prison, and did not help you?' He will reply, 'I tell you *the truth, whatever you did not do for one of the least of these, you did not do for me.'"* (Matt. 25:37–40, 44, 45)

Martin the Cobbler is a powerful claymation video based on a story from Leo Tolstoy's *Where Love Is, There God Is Also*. After the unexpected death of his wife and baby, Martin stops believing God cares for him. One day the local priest visits his shop and asks Martin to repair the leather binding on a Bible, secretly hoping Martin will read it. And that's just what happens. Martin falls asleep reading it, and in a dream, God says to him, "Tomorrow I will visit you, Martin."[5]

The next day Martin wakes excitedly. He cleans and prepares for his very important guest. He works with enthusiasm and checks often through the window waiting for his guest to arrive. However, the only person he sees is a lonely lamplighter making his rounds in the frigid air. Martin invites him in for a warming cup of tea.

After he leaves, Martin notices a young mother nearby in a thin shawl, desperately trying to shield her baby from the cold. Martin invites them in to share his soup and bread, then bestows on them gifts—his wife's shawl and his child's tiny pair of shoes.

When they leave Martin again gazes out the window and sees a boy stealing an apple from an old woman. He runs to catch the thief, but instead of berating him as the old woman has begun to do, he helps them see each other as potential friends. The boy is hungry and needs food desperately; the woman is old and needs someone to carry her apples home for her. Once the woman and boy establish a friendship, Martin sends them on their way.

Now it's growing dark and people are going inside for the night. Martin is sad and angry that God hasn't kept his promise to visit him that day. He again falls asleep reading the Bible and asking, "Why didn't you come?"

God answers him, using the words of the parable he's been reading, "If you have done it unto the least of these, Martin, you have done it unto me. I was the lamplighter whom you warmed with hot tea. I was the mother and child you fed and clothed. I was the boy and the old woman. I *did* visit you, Martin."

Martin knew heartache and had succumbed to grief and bitterness, but Jesus loved him enough to reassure him that he had, indeed, visited him that very day. Martin was able to release his painful feelings and learn to give and receive love once again.

Like many, my life is full of stuff to do: lessons to prepare, appointments to keep, food to fix, and clothes to wash. Who has time to stop and look for more opportunities to serve? These verses remind me that when I show compassion to a wounded child, I am hugging Jesus. When I listen sympathetically to a lonely woman at the grocery store, I'm listening to Jesus. When I clean at the Women's Shelter, I'm cleaning a place where Jesus lives. Too often I forget this amazing truth.

For me, the "least of these" are frequently the children in my classroom, the ones I keep stumbling over in my struggle to get through the urgent demands of daily life. I can make my plans a priority and push aside or slight my children, or I can choose to care for them as I would care for Jesus.

O, Lord, I'm cut to the heart by this parable! The least are the greatest in your eyes, greater than anything else I might hope to get done today. My children's needs are more important than crossing off another item on my list. Teach me how to schedule my time and energy so I can be open to opportunities to serve them and also be available to others. Help me to watch for ways to love people as if they were you. Amen.

11

Following Jesus' Example

When he had finished washing their feet, he put on his clothes, and returned to his place. "Do you understand what I have done for you?" he asked them. "You call me 'Teacher' and 'Lord,' and rightly so, for that is what I am. Now that I, your Lord and Teacher, have washed your feet, you also should wash one another's feet. I have set you an example that you should do as I have done for you. I tell you the truth, no servant is greater than his master, nor is a messenger greater than the one who sent him. Now

that you know these things, you will be blessed if you do them."
(John 13:12–17)

"Do you understand what I have done for you?" What a penetrating question Jesus asked.

Yes, I know the Son of God himself came down from heaven and lived in human flesh. He died an excruciating, humiliating death to pay the penalty for my sins and then rose again on the third day. Now he sits at the right hand of the Father until the day he returns for his children. I know all that, but I'm not sure I understand all of it. I feel like one of Jesus' disciples, dumbfounded that the Master would stoop to wash dirty feet.

Jesus' next words continually unsettle me, "You call me 'Teacher' and 'Lord,' and rightly so, for that is what I am." It's true; I do call him by those titles. He is that and so much more. Why then, if I acknowledge him as the Teacher above all teachers, don't I come to him with all my questions? If he's Lord and Master over all, why don't I bow down before him all the time?

Jesus continues, "Now that I, your Lord and Teacher, have washed your feet, you also should wash one another's feet. I have set you an example that you should do as I have done for you."

You mean, be a *servant* to others? Then I begin thinking: *Well, it might be fine for you, Jesus. After all that's why you came. But*

I'm not good at that sort of thing. I have a sensitive nose, a weak stomach, and I'm allergic to dirt.

Just who do I think I am if I'm not Christ's servant? I volunteered for this work when I surrendered my life to him. The hard part comes when others treat me as a servant. I must remember that in serving others, I also serve him.

Then Jesus brings his message home, "Now that you know these things, you will be blessed if you do them." The blessing isn't in simply knowing God's will, but in doing it. I tend to turn that around. Knowing to do right is worthless without obedience.

I've participated in several foot-washing services. Each occasion was beautiful and symbolic. In Jesus' day it was not only good hospitality, but also a necessary function in the dusty, sandal-clad times in which he lived. But Jesus' lesson for his disciples, both then and now, is not just about being hospitable or cleaning feet. Jesus demonstrated that a servant is gracious, always responding to the needs of the moment.

As homeschool moms we must choose to extend simple, gracious hospitality to others, showing flexibility to serve when needs arise. Whether we're cleaning, doing yard work at the church, taking food to families under stress, or pulling weeds from a neighbor's lawn—this is foot washing of the twenty-first century. We will be blessed as we put it into practice.

Dear God, you know I really don't want to wash anyone else's feet. Show me how to surrender this attitude to you, and allow me to be of service where I'm most needed. Help me not to turn up my nose when faced with unpleasant tasks. Create in me a willingness to roll up my sleeves, get down on my knees, and work hard. Grant me a spirit of humility and a sincere love for the ones I'm serving. Amen.

12

Who's Wielding the Ax?

If the ax is dull and its edge unsharpened, more strength is needed but skill will bring success. (Eccl. 10:10)

In the book of Judges, the angel of the Lord assures Gideon he wants him to lead the people into battle. Gideon is flabbergasted. "But I'm from the weakest clan and I'm the least in my family," he whimpers.

The Lord responds to Gideon: "I will be with you and you will strike down all the Midianites together" (Judg. 6:16). It didn't matter to God that Gideon was weak and the least in his family—God planned to show his power through Gideon.

Ecclesiastes 10:10 says that if the blade is dull, more strength is needed to do the work. There's no one stronger than God. He brought the whole universe into being, needing only to speak it into existence. He holds lightning in his hands and sends waves crashing on the shore. He both delivers and withholds the rain. God gives us our very breath. His strength is unmatched.

The verse also says that if the edge of an ax is unsharpened, only skill will bring success. At times homeschooling feels like hacking at a hardwood tree with an unsharpened, dull blade. Progress seems slow, even though we're giving it all we've got. We may not be the sharpest knives in the drawer, but if God has chosen us as his tools it doesn't matter what we might think.

When Gideon raised an army to go against the Midianites, God told him to send some of them home. "You have too many men for me to deliver Midian into [your] hands. In order that Israel may not boast against me that [your] own strength has saved [you]" (Judg. 7:2).

That's the key. Our efforts can never compare to God's, even if we do our best and avail ourselves of every resource. He wants to make sure we know he's the One doing the work through us.

Imagine an ax boasting that it felled a forest of trees by itself. Of course, we know that an ax would be useless without the woodsman who aimed each mighty blow.

Over and over again, God chooses to use people that others would have passed by. "But God chose the foolish things of the world to shame the wise; God chose the weak things of the world to shame the strong. He chose the lowly things of this world and the despised things—and the things that are not—to nullify the things that are, so that no one may boast before him" (1 Cor. 1:27–29).

Are you feeling a little dull around the edges lately? You don't have to hold a doctorate in education or theology to successfully teach your children. God just wants you to put yourself in his hands and let him do the work.

God, I know my weaknesses. They are too many to count. I'm not as sharp as I'd like to be, but I'm available. I want to keep learning so you can use me to accomplish your will. You have the strength and the skills I don't possess. In order to succeed I need you to work in me and through me. And when victory comes help me remember who's responsible for it, that I may boast only in you. Amen.

13

The Yoke's on Us

"Come to me, all you who are weary and burdened, and I will give you rest. Take my yoke upon you and learn from me, for I am gentle and humble in heart, and you will find rest for your souls. For my yoke is easy and my burden is light." (Matt. 11:28–30)

We laughed until we cried as our four daughters, inside a single hula hoop, ran back and forth across my sister's yard. They called it their "hoop skirt," changing direction according to the whims of whichever girl had the strongest will at that moment. They looked like drunken sailors weaving all over the yard. They were comically yoked.

Jesus invites us to share his yoke, not so we can entertain the world with our antics but so

46

14

According to Your Ability

"It will be like a man going on a journey, who called his servants and entrusted his property to them. To one he gave five talents of money, to another two talents, and to another one talent, each according to his ability. Then he went on his journey." (Matt. 25:14, 15)

The talents Jesus talks about in this parable can be interpreted three ways: our skills, our spiritual gifts, or our money. In any case the message is to be a good steward of what God gives us, whether it's musical talent, athletic ability, effective prayer, evangelistic enthusiasm, or wealth.

In Jesus' parable each servant was gifted according to his ability and was judged on how he handled his talent.

At times I find myself comparing my talents to the talents of others. Result: I always seem to come up short. I wanted to be an athlete in school, but no matter how hard I worked I just didn't have the natural ability others had. I see a writer whose books are published regularly and wonder, *Why isn't that me?* And I'm constantly amazed at the energy and perseverance I see in many homeschooling teachers. They tackle science projects with gusto, manage to read stacks of books with their kids, and still finish the school year on time.

God doesn't give us talents to feed our egos, however. His plan is to teach us obedience. So if I receive only the one talent of being a good teacher while author Max Lucado receives ten talents, I am still a success in God's eyes if I multiply my talent. He doesn't expect any more than that from me.

God created the lilac, the rose, and the hyacinth to be beautiful and fragrant, while he created grapevines, strawberry plants, and apricot trees to produce fruit. Each plant produces according to its design and ability. It would be silly for a bean plant to hide her blossoms simply because she's not as pretty as the rose. Miss Bean compares her plain white blossoms to Miss Rose's velvety petals and feels inadequate. She forgets that beauty can't satisfy a hungry tummy.

Have you "bean" there, bemoaning your lack of talents? Do you compare your talent to the talents of others? Maybe you're not as beautiful as a movie star, or you can't cook gourmet meals. Maybe you can't carry a tune to save your life, and the thought of another unit study makes you weary. What has God given you the ability to do?

God gives each of us different talents for a purpose. They may not always be flashy, but they fit us—our personality, circumstances, and place in time. Each individual's portion is perfectly suited to him or her. God doesn't make mistakes.

Our job is to take the talents God has given us and produce eternal results for his Kingdom. We should not squander them or hide them because we think they are insignificant. We are to use our talents to bring honor to him—nothing more and nothing less.

Dear Jesus, forgive my ungratefulness for believing my talents are few and not as desirable as those you've given others. I'm relieved I don't have to compete with other homeschooling teachers, or with anyone else. Praise your holy name! What a joy to know I can be myself and still please you. Amen.

15

Being Useful

Formerly he was useless to you, but now he has become useful both to you and to me. (Philem. 11)

Philemon is one of the shortest books in the Bible, but tucked away inside it is an eloquent message on usefulness. Paul writes this letter to Philemon, a fellow believer, on behalf of Onesimus, a runaway slave. Paul has been instrumental in Onesimus's conversion to Christianity and the two have became friends. Over time, Onesimus desires to return to Philemon, but fears for his life, since runaway slaves can be put to death. In his personal letter to Philemon, Paul tells him that Onesimus is now a brother in Christ—he (Onesimus) is no longer a possession.

He goes on to say that Onesimus, whose name means "useful," has been a tremendous help to him and wishes to return and be a useful servant to Philemon as well. Paul asks Philemon to show kindness and forgive Onesimus.

I root for Onesimus when I read this letter. "Philemon, please be merciful," my heart cries. "He's changed. Really he has." I hold such high hopes for him, because I've been there too. I've run from God, rebelling against his authority and fearing punishment for my disobedience. When I chose to follow Jesus, God took me into his household and gave me a place to serve. Being useful to him affects me profoundly and impacts every aspect of my life.

The Bible has quite a bit to say about usefulness.

My work is meaningful. "[Do] something useful with [your] own hands, that [you] may have something to share with those in need" (Eph. 4:28).

Work is not always something we do with our hands, but I believe homeschooling to be a definite hands-on profession. I delegate certain parts of my job to others, such as music instruction, gymnastics, and riding lessons, yet it's still my overall job to ensure my children receive a great education.

I do not earn a salary for this work; however, innumerable benefits come with my role as a homeschool teacher. When opportunities to serve others arise, I can give to them in ways that I would not be able to if I worked outside my home. For instance, I can bake goodies for a friend experiencing a tough time, or open my home to someone in need of shelter, or even help educate others about homeschooling and assist them in getting started. I can do all these things and so many others while I am at "work."

My faith is useful if it affects my actions. "Do you want evidence that faith without deeds is useless?" (James 2:20).

Turn that verse into a positive statement: "Faith that produces action is useful." This is one of the greatest benefits of homeschooling my children. It's up close and personal, and if I'm not living what I teach or practicing what I preach, they'll certainly call me on it. It keeps me on my knees before God.

The Bible is a useful tool. "All Scripture is God-breathed and is useful for teaching, rebuking, correcting and training in righteousness" (2 Tim. 3:16).

This is what a homeschool teacher's job is all about: teaching, correcting, and training our children in righteousness. Only the Word of God has life-changing power, so all the lecturing in the world about letting go of bad habits or of being a good person will be useless without the Bible backing me up. It's my job to share the life-giving words of God himself; then he can do the rest.

I can be a valuable vessel. "In a well-furnished kitchen there are not only crystal goblets and silver platters, but waste cans and compost buckets—some containers used to serve fine meals, others to take out the garbage. Become the kind of container God can use to present any and every kind of gift to his guests for their blessing" (2 Tim. 2:20, 21, *The Message*).

Once I was a common, ordinary vessel that bore the scars of rough handling, but when I chose to serve God, all that changed. He lovingly reshaped me into a vessel of pure silver and gold—one that cannot be broken or destroyed. He cleansed me and refined me, and now I'm useful to him. He's not ashamed to claim me as his own, and I'm not ashamed of myself either.

I have a useful faith. "And if Christ has not been raised, our preaching is useless and so is your faith" (1 Cor. 15:14).

Because Christ was raised from the dead, our teaching and our faith are useful (of value, helpful, worthy). The message of Christ is real; therefore, my faith rests on a rock-solid foundation. It's only through that faith I am able to survive times of doubt and despair.

In serving only the Master, my work, my actions, my words, my witness, and my faith are useful to God every day. He's brought meaning and purpose into my life, even on the toughest days.

Don't even think about running away!

Lord and Master, I've chosen to follow you. Remind me daily that I serve you, and show me how you want to use me in our school today. Show me how I can be useful to my fellow brothers and sisters in Christ and also to those around me who do not know you. Let those who serve in your household look to you for guidance and be encouraged to live useful lives. Amen.

16

An Inheritance

"So now I charge you in the sight of all Israel and of the assembly of the LORD and in the hearing of our God: Be careful to follow all the commands of the LORD your God, that you may possess this good land and pass it on as an inheritance to your descendants forever." (1 Chron. 28:8)

The day after my grandpa's funeral, my sister and I went to his home with Mom and Dad. Mom stood in the center of the room holding a box, not quite ready to face the painful task of sorting through his personal effects. "You girls look around and see what you'd like to have to remember Grandpa."

We glanced around halfheartedly. What did we want? Grandpa's life was our inheritance. Our hearts overflowed with memories of his funny jokes, his fascinating stories, and all the toys and furniture he'd made for us over the years. I cherished an old cassette tape that had captured his gravelly voice telling us his life story. And last Christmas he'd typed up copies of the story about how he and Grandma came out west from Nebraska during the Great Depression. Proudly, he gave each of us a copy. What could I possibly treasure more than these, more than my grandpa himself?

What did I want? I claimed the maple desk chair, one of his shirts to wear around the house, and a few bottles of craft paint, but again, Grandpa had already given me my inheritance. He'd left me a lifetime of watching him put his faith in God into action.

Grandpa Johnston had obeyed three charges given to the Israelites centuries before:

First, he'd followed all the commands of the Lord. This was evident at his memorial service. Friend after friend shared how Grandpa's honesty and integrity had inspired them.

Second, he possessed the land. Grandpa claimed his home and family for God and fought all of his life to keep the enemy from encroaching on that inheritance.

Finally, he passed his godly inheritance on to his descendants. His two daughters, Joanne and Mary, inherited his faith and passed it on to their six children. And now we're passing it on to our seven children. We pray that they, in turn, will bequeath this heirloom of faith to their children.

Perhaps you share the same sort of joy from being a third-, fourth-, or fifth-generation Christian. If you're the first believer in your family, congratulations! All future generations will inherit from you. It's up to you to "possess the land" for your family.

Here are two practical ways you can pass on this inheritance:

1) Follow all of God's commands, not just the ones you like or find easy to obey. You are an example of righteousness to your children in every facet of your life: in words, in deeds, in compassion, in honesty, in devotional time, and in personal witnessing.

2) Be a lifelong student of the Bible, and plant a desire for God's Word in your children's hearts. Use colorful Bible stories, and then advance to Bible studies and devotionals to help them grasp God's truth on their level. Seeing you excited about studying the Bible yourself will make a lasting impression.

Passing on this inheritance to the next generation is the best part. As adults we're war heroes with stories to tell. We can sprinkle our life adventures into classes on literature, history, and the Bible. Even our failures can make for better strategic planning to help defeat the enemy. Our children will benefit from our past knowledge as they fight against the wiles of the devil. They'll need both offensive and defensive weapons to win this war, and those weapons are the Word of God and prayer.

How exciting it is to possess a family treasure that won't wear out, won't lose its value, and won't be removed from us, except by sharing. In fact, in giving it away it only becomes more valuable!

Dear Commander in Chief, let me leave an inheritance worth passing on to the next generation. You alone know of all the missed opportunities, all the battles lost. You alone know how much it has cost to gain even this small piece of ground I have claimed for you. Make me determined to follow you, Lord, in order to defeat the enemy and possess the land. I want to leave a lasting legacy for those who follow this way. Amen.

17

Playing Favorites

The boys grew up, and Esau became a skillful hunter, a man of the open country, while Jacob was a quiet man, staying among the tents. Isaac, who had a taste for wild game, loved Esau, but Rebekah loved Jacob. (Gen. 25:27, 28)

Whenever parents favor one child over another there's bound to be competition, rejection, and sorrow for everyone involved. It's even worse when parents choose a favorite child and use him to manipulate and plot against the other! And yet it's an easy thing to do.

How many times have you heard the "always and never" speech from your children?

"You love him more than you love me. She always gets to do everything and I never get to do anything!"

Your decision has little or nothing to do with favoritism. Most likely, it's based on the amount of money in your purse at the time, or how well that particular child was behaving. Sometimes it's just because you're tired, and *no* naturally rolls off your tongue.

Picture this biblical family. Father Isaac is a huntin' and fishin' sort of guy. He loves the smell of the great outdoors. Son Esau's fiery red hair, ruddy complexion, and essence of sweat signal manhood to Isaac. Esau works magic when it comes to wild game . . . why, it makes Isaac's stomach growl just thinking about it.

Rebekah, however, spends her time at home. Jacob is such a comfort to her with his quiet ways and gentle manner. He smells of soap and fresh baked bread, not sweat and dirty animal skins.

Do you have one child who's easier to love and spend time with? Do you have a child who continually gets on your nerves? Do you have to work harder to think of positive things to say to him or her? Are you tired of constantly correcting one specific child? Do you restrain yourself from choking this one child? And does your spouse secretly prefer one youngster?

Isaac and Rebekah each had their favorite son, and they didn't keep it a secret. Instead, they chose sides and used their sons to take potshots at each other. We can prevent this from occurring in our families by following a few simple, albeit difficult, steps.

Talk openly to God if you find yourself playing favorites among your children. The Lord already knows your feelings, so the confession won't shock him. Sincere prayer opens the door to God's response. He can then give you the ammunition you need to overcome this temptation.

Second, go on a treasure hunt. Look for evidence of God in your child's life. Thank God for creating this special youngster, and ask God how his or her annoying characteristics can be used for future good.

Last, but not least, find things to praise and encourage in your child. Cover their school papers with smiley faces or compliments whenever you can. Leave a loving, tender greeting card on their desk. Take time to bake their favorite treat, or plan an outing for just the two of you. When you're alone together, ask about his or her dreams, fears, and disappointments.

In order for true learning to occur, children must feel valued and hopeful about their future. That's a big advantage of homeschooling, because only a parent cares that much. Seize every opportunity to show your children Christlike love. God can keep us from repeating Isaac and Rebekah's mistakes.

Lord God, stop me from showing favoritism among my children. When I fail, forgive me and show me ways to seek their forgiveness as well. Let me hear my words from their perspectives, and give me strength when I'm tempted to show preference to one over the other. Help me be more like you, Lord. I'm so thankful that you don't play favorites. Amen.

18

A Burden for
the Weary

*"The images that are carried about are burdensome, a
burden for the weary . . . Listen to me . . . you whom I
have upheld since you were conceived, and have carried since your birth. Even to your old age and gray
hairs I am he, I am he who will sustain you. I have
made you and I will carry you; I will sustain you and
I will rescue you . . . I am God, and there is no other; I
am God, and there is none like me."* (Isa. 46:1–4, 9)

Did you read the foreword to this book?
C'mon, be honest. If you didn't, I'd like you to
go back now and read it. It's a skit that illustrates the theme of this section, *My God Carries*

Me. By reading the foreword, this devotion will make a lot more sense to you.

* * *

The skit in the foreword is not the most profound drama in mankind's history, but it illustrates the truth that we serve a God who carries *us,* not the other way around. Much of the time, we miss this radical concept.

Like the title character Pilgrim in *Pilgrim's Progress,* we've surrendered our lives and accepted Christ's sacrifice on the cross, transferring our burden of sin to him. However, problems remain. When we again load ourselves down with regrets over what might have been, should have been, or ought to have been, the load can feel many times heavier than the one we originally gave to the Lord. It takes place so gradually that we're unaware of what's happening until we stagger under its weight. I believe this is where we venture into the land of idolatry. *The American Heritage Dictionary* defines the word "idol" as:

1. *An image used as an object of worship. A false god.*
2. *A person or thing that is blindly or excessively adored.*
3. *Something visible but without substance.*[7]

The first definition is probably not an issue. I don't know any Christians who worship idols. However, numbers two and three cause me to squirm a little. An idol can be something excessively adored and/or without substance. I can think of more than a few things I adore that have no substance.

For instance, I crave praise from others for my involvement in ministry. It soothes my insecurities. I love the attention that homeschooling the girls gives me and our family. I'm so infatuated with doing things that feed my self-worth, that I get over involved doing busy things (often, with no substance). I'm passionate about being busy. It's almost an unholy devotion. Just admitting it in this chapter is humiliating enough.

Recently Launa confided in me about a problem she was having with a friend. I opened my mouth to give her some sage, motherly advice and then promptly shut it again. I envisioned myself dragging around a little idol called Human Wisdom, thinking I had all the answers. Instantly, I banished the idolatrous thoughts. Instead Launa and I prayed for God's wisdom in her situation.

By doing this, Launa learned to take her problems straight to God. Whereas I was all gung-ho to hoist an idol of human wisdom on my back, God stepped in and reminded me to drop it at his feet. That day Launa and I both learned anew a valuable lesson. God wants us to lay our idols (and gods) at his feet. He wants to be the God who carries us and not the other way around.

O, God, you are God, the one true God! How wonderful that you don't expect me to carry the burden of my salvation around in backpacks of sacrifice, good works, and legalistic rule keeping. Your death freed me to live a life of faith and dependence upon you. Continue to remind me that you need no help carrying any load. In the name of Jesus, I offer this prayer. Amen.

19

Jesus Is Praying for You

"Satan has asked to sift you as wheat. But I have prayed for you . . . that your faith may not fail. And when you have turned back, strengthen your brothers." (Luke 22:31, 32)

I'm always heartened to know others are praying for me, and especially when they ask *how* they can pray for me. Knowing that another believer is lifting up my name and my needs before God blesses me immeasurably. I feel like I'm Moses on the mountaintop, during the battle with the Amalekites, with Aaron holding my arm up on one side and Hur holding up the arm on the opposite side, keeping the victory rod high and allowing me to defeat my personal "Amalekites" (enemies).

Then there are those days when I feel completely forgotten. People promise to pray, but they forget . . . I know, I know, they're only human. They plan to pray, but they get preoccupied with other things. Maybe my prayer request is misunderstood and my need is missed entirely. Or they forget to pray at all until something jogs their memory, but by then the need has passed.

So, imagine how Peter must have felt when Jesus informed him that he had been praying for him. Jesus prayed for Peter's upcoming temptation, not just for his current circumstances. Wow! None of my friends have ever said to me:

"Hey, Beth, Satan's going to do a number on you today and try to convince you that you're a terrible teacher and your kids aren't learning a thing from you. So, I've prayed for you. You're not only going to triumph over the devil, but your experience will encourage other homeschoolers as well."

Jesus prayed for Peter, and he continues to intercede for us today. He stands as our Advocate before the Father, constantly asking God to move against Satan and his plans to destroy a believer's faith. He asks the Father to strengthen us with wisdom, courage, and perseverance in all trials so that we may resist temptation and bring glory to God. Only Jesus knows the personal demons that plague each of us, even the ones we dare not tell to anyone. Our Savior's prayer gives us the victory and allows us an experience in which we can then minister to others. No one knows what someone else may be feeling or going through quite like someone who's already been there.

That's the kind of prayer warrior I want rooting for me! Today I feel like a child's ball, tossed back and forth between kids until I'm dizzy and dazed. I'm dejected and unsure the girls are learning anything. All day long, they have quarreled with each other. It seems I'm fighting a losing battle with the dog for their attention.

Jesus knew I'd have days like this, so he's already asked God to provide me with a win. What a tremendous joy and relief to be backed by that kind of intercessor.

Be encouraged! Jesus is praying for you. You will make it through this day, this week, this year—enabled by his power. Lean on him. He's your blue-ribbon, prayer warrior.

Jesus, you are King of kings and Lord of lords, and yet you are my Chief Intercessor and are continuously bringing my needs before the Father. How awesome it is to call you Savior. At this moment, I picture you seated in Heaven on the Father's right-hand side, gently and sweetly discussing my concerns with him. Thank you for loving me. I've no doubt I'll triumph with you on my side! Amen.

20

In the Ravine

"You will drink from the brook, and I have ordered the ravens to feed you there." (1 Kings 17:4)

These particular words of Scripture affect me profoundly because I go through periods of "drought." Even though blessings surround me and my homeschool teaching is going great, I sometimes feel so dry inside.

Several years ago I penned these thoughts in my journal:

> *Oh, to hide away in a ravine and drink from the brook of God, where he would feed me and renew my strength. I need you, Lord.*

I don't know where this dissatisfaction comes from, those distractions that pull me away from true worship. They are all around and I am tired of beating them off to get to you. I am weary of trying to worship. Take me to a place where I can be alone with you, be fed by your Word, and hear your voice clearly. Oh, how I need to hear your voice! (9/19/98)

As I reread this entry the same feelings flood my heart, and I cry out to him again. My duties are stifling me, and all I want to do is break away and spend time with him. Soon my retreat will be here, and I'll have three glorious days to do just that.

Every year in winter, when the world seems bleakest, I get away to take time for myself. Three days of doing only what I want to do: shopping, writing, taking long walks on the beach, eating ridiculously, staying in my pajamas, and most important, communing with the Lord in prayer and praise. I don't have to worry about the phone ringing, the dog needing to go out, or my family's needs. Hooray! It's just God and me, and we have a marvelous time. When it's over, I leave refreshed, nourished by the Word, and ready to go back to my everyday life. I'm happy to see my family and begin afresh.

It's important for homeschool teachers to have a scheduled time away from their teaching environment. I feel strongly about taking a short break from teaching. I may not walk through the doors of a highly stressful business every day, but I still need to recharge my batteries. Being alone with the Lord is a great rejuvenator.

If your life seems a little parched right now, maybe it's time to retreat and spend time with the Lord. Even if you have only a short while, you can make it count and come away revitalized. Take a walk during lunch or after dinner—make this time a quiet mini-retreat. Weather permitting, drive to a neighborhood park, soak up some rays on a bench, and enjoy God's presence and nature's lovely ambiance.

Whatever your situation God knows all about it, and he can find a way for the two of you to get together. He'll provide the ravine, the brook, and the ravens. All you have to do is come willingly.

Lord, Creator of the universe, I worship you and need so much more of you, but time is always short. Provide me with time and a quiet place without interruption, so I may feed my soul with your Word. Quench my thirsting soul, Father, and thank you for making a way for me to be with you. Amen.

21

Like a Scarecrow in a Melon Patch

Hear what the Lord says to you . . . "For the customs of the peoples are worthless; they cut a tree out of the forest, and a craftsman shapes it with his chisel. They adorn it with silver and gold; they fasten it with hammer and nails so it will not totter. Like a scarecrow in a melon patch, their idols cannot speak; they must be carried because they cannot walk. Do not fear them; they can do no harm nor can they do any good. No one is like you, O LORD; you are great, and your name is mighty in power." (Jer. 10:1–6)

All I can do is laugh when I read about these poor, deluded people securing their wooden idols in order to keep them from falling flat on their wooden faces. It reminds me of the marvelous scene in 1 Samuel 5, where Dagon, god of the Philistines, ends up facedown before the ark of the Lord. This is a god worthy of worship? A god made of wood, dressed up in precious metals, and carted around by mere mortals? I don't think so! Why worship some object that is inanimate?

Vine's Expository Dictionary of Old and New Testament Words says, "'Demons' are the spiritual agents acting in all idolatry. The idol itself is nothing, but every idol has a 'demon' associated with it who induces idolatry, with its worship and sacrifices."[8] That's what entices people to worship a man-made object with such fervor and sacrifice, the demon behind the scarecrow.

Demons have very limited power, though, and God tells us not to fear the power of the enemy, but rather, to fear him who has power over life or death. Demons tremble before God (see James 2:19); they recognize Christ as their future Judge (see Matt. 8:29, Luke 4:41). Jesus cast them out of people by his own power, and his disciples were able to cast them out in his name, by faith (see Matt. 17:19, 20).

In his book, *The Annals of a Satanist,* Frank Alvarez III relates his firsthand experience of God's supreme power in this dimension. Frank had pursued a relationship with Satan for most of his life, but God reached him with a Bible placed strategically in his path at just the right time. By faith, Frank set out to find God. One day, after giving his testimony for the first time in church, Frank came home and sensed a familiar dark presence:

> Frank's mind fought hard to keep calm and think rationally, but all of the training in the world could not prepare someone for the presence of such evil. Subconsciously he realized that he was in a fetal position. He did not move an inch; he only waited . . . Frank's soul wanted to fight. Suddenly, and to his surprise, he began to speak in a calm, gentle tone that carried the strength of all of the power of the universe.
>
> "Satan, I do not belong to you anymore, I belong to Jesus. I found out the truth, and you have to go away now because you do not belong here anymore. I am no longer yours, I don't love you anymore, so you go away" . . . He knew the power he felt could only be the Spirit that God gives to those who come to know him. Thanking Jesus in his heart, Frank closed his eyes and rested.[9]

Much energy has been spent in recent years to educate the church about demons and the occult. That's a good thing. As homeschoolers, we also must teach our children about the battle believers are engaged in every day. The enemy is devious and strong. However, when we cling to the One who loves us, we have nothing to fear. The name of Jesus is enough to send demons fleeing in terror. Compared to God, Satan and his idols are just so many scarecrows in a melon patch. It's a battle doomed to failure, and Satan knows it.

Dearest Lord, I don't want to be ignorant of the devil's schemes. Neither do I want to focus too much attention on him, fearing his influence over my children. Give me ideas for lesson plans that will show my children how to be as wise as serpents and yet as innocent as doves. Fill each of us with your holy power, and let righteousness overcome evil. Amen.

22

Cords of Kindness

"When Israel was a child, I loved him, and out of Egypt I called my son. But the more I called Israel, the further they went from me. They sacrificed to the Baals and they burned incense to images. It was I who taught Ephraim to walk, taking them by the arms; but they did not realize it was I who healed them. I led them with cords of human kindness, with ties of love; I lifted the yoke from their neck and bent down to feed them." (Hos. 11:1–4)

Wow, what a passage! The father heart of God is perfectly described as he interacts with his people. Just look at all the wonderful descriptive verbs in these verses: loved, called, taught, healed, led, lifted, and bent down. No one can say we serve an impersonal God.

But wait, what about those wayward children of Israel? The more God called them, the farther away they ran. They showered their love on inanimate objects and gave others credit for every good thing that came their way.

Sound familiar? Parenting can be such a thankless job sometimes. Whenever I call my girls and they turn a deaf ear, listening only for words like ice cream or McDonald's, it hurts me. It's called selective hearing and all children have it, a sort of built-in radar system for kids. They shower love on objects—toys, dolls, bicycles, the telephone, the computer, and television—and I feel neglected.

Someone else always seems to be getting credit for what I teach them. For years, I've tried to get my girls to wash their hands before meals, brush their teeth before bed, and a myriad of other tasks. But it's not until they hear it from their Grandma, the youth pastor, or from one of their friends that they suddenly "see the light." You'd think they'd actually had a special revelation.

God says, "I led them with cords of human kindness." The word *cord* intrigues me. Some Bible commentaries and dictionaries give the analogy of a man leading an ox with a rope. Somehow that just doesn't fit my image of a loving parent. Instead, I picture an umbilical cord.

It's a life-giving source to the baby while growing inside the womb, providing nourishment during the development before birth. Even when the cord is severed, the bellybutton remains as a lifelong reminder of the connection once shared by mother and child. In the same fashion, God's cord of human kindness is one that nourishes us, provides for us, and reminds us of his role as our heavenly Father.

Unlike Israel, I choose not to be the bratty kid that runs away every time I hear my Father calling. I choose to respond positively even when I don't like what he has to say. After all, He is the only reason I exist on this planet, so he surely deserves my attention.

This Scripture shows what a great example God is as a parent. He doesn't grab us by the seat of the pants and haul us off to the woodshed for an up close and personal view of corporal punishment. Oh no, not our God! Instead, he uses the same cord of loving kindness to *woo* us back to him, and he inspires me to do the same with my children.

Wooing is definitely more effective than forcing, as Charles Swindoll relates in *Quest for Character:*

> I often picture those in the early church as being people of contagious charm. Whenever that mental picture appears, the insightful words of Reinhold Niebuhr come to my mind:
>
> "You may be able to compel people to maintain certain minimum standards by stressing duty, but the highest moral and spiritual achievements depend not upon a push but a pull. People must be charmed into righteousness."[10]

I couldn't agree more!

Lord, may I become a parent and teacher after your example—patient, loving, and faithful. Help me to model your ideal, and show me ways to woo my children closer to us both. Stop me when I resort to force, to try to get them to obey. I also ask you to help me become a more obedient child myself—willing to listen and full of gratitude and praise for you. Amen.

23

Hindrances

He said to another person, "Come, be my disciple." The man agreed, but he said, "Lord, first let me return home and bury my father." Jesus replied, "Let those who are spiritually dead care for their own dead. Your duty is to go and preach the coming of the Kingdom of God."

Another said, "Yes, Lord, I will follow you, but first let me say good-bye to my family." But Jesus told him, "Anyone who puts a hand to the plow and then looks back is not fit for the Kingdom of God." (Luke 9:59–62 NLT)

Jesus asks two different men to follow him and become his disciples. Both men want to follow Jesus, but both have excuses for why they can't follow him right at that time. One man wants to wait until his father dies and the other wants an opportunity to say good-bye to his family. Apparently, neither man is ready to forsake family ties in order to follow Christ. The answer Jesus gives them leaves no doubt as to where their loyalties should lie—if you decide to follow me (put your hand to the plow) and then decide it's too hard (look back) then you're really not a candidate for God's Kingdom.

Jamieson, Fausset and Brown Bible Commentary states,

> Ploughing [plowing] requires an eye intent on the furrow to be made, and is marred the instant one turns about . . . This man's problem was not an *actual return* to the world, but a *reluctance to break with it.*[11]

Whether you plan on being your children's sole educator, or if you're homeschooling for only a season, maybe you are doing it because God has called you to it. Perhaps you felt compelled in the midst of reading his Word or while watching your child struggle in a traditional school setting. Maybe you don't live close to an acceptable school, and private education is not affordable. In my case I was called to home education through the voice of my child. There are many reasons to homeschool, but whatever your reasons, never doubt you are fulfilling God's purpose.

Will my furrow be straight? Or will it be crooked because I'm selfishly preoccupied? Everywhere I look—distractions. Worldly distractions that beg me "come"!

Any preoccupation, even momentarily, that leads me away from my primary goal needs to be dealt with.

Shopping is just one such distraction for me. So as I'm out and about I begin thinking: Tara needs new shoes. Oh, and while I'm out, I might as well pick up a birthday gift for Josie. And I know Jeff needs some new shirts. Pretty soon the afternoon's shot and I haven't cracked open a book all day.

Housework is another major distraction. I can't afford a maid, so I brace myself for endless rounds of dirty dishes, smelly laundry, and other, seemingly, never-ending chores.

Top it off with commitments to church, Bible studies, and hobbies—all beckoning me like Greek sirens luring unsuspecting sailors to their doom.

Now, I'm not implying there is no life until after the kids are grown and gone—far from it. What I am saying is that too often these other matters serve to veer me off course, and that once perfectly straight furrow I've been happily plowing is looking more and more like the Grand Canyon. Homeschooling is my calling; the other stuff is extra. I need to fit it in around my teaching hours.

If your furrow is looking pretty ragged lately, lay it at the Lord's feet and let him weed out the distractions for you. Let him also bless you with friendships and activities nourishing to your soul and energizing to your spirit. Field hands do get lunch breaks and an occasional rest in the shade. Your furrow is the only one you have to plow, so give it your all.

Dear Jesus, I've accepted your call and I'm willing to serve, but I do get distracted at times. Teaching my children at home is one of the biggest responsibilities you've given me, and I realize its importance. Sure, there are many activities I'd like to be involved in, but I know homeschooling is not an extra. Help me keep my furrow straight and my eyes on the goal. Help me keep my hand to the plow. I love you, Lord. Amen.

24

Downward Spiral

After Rehoboam's position as king was established and he had become strong, he and all Israel with him abandoned the law of the LORD. . . . He did evil because he had not set his heart on seeking the LORD. (2 Chron. 12:1, 14)

Jill and Tanya were best friends through grade school and junior high. Occasionally, Tanya would get excited about serving God and going to church, but it wasn't long before she lost interest in spiritual things. She allowed boys and the dating life to become her god.

Jill's love for the Lord, on the other hand, grew steadily; it wasn't long before she and Tanya drifted apart. In college, Jill was thrilled to hear that Tanya, as well as her boyfriend, had rededicated their lives to the Lord. Both glowed with an inner radiance that convinced Jill it would last.

But the following summer Tanya's life was blown apart when her mother announced that she and Tanya's father were getting a divorce after twenty-five years of marriage. She said she'd never really loved Tanya's dad and had only married him to get away from home. Each family member reacted differently. Tanya's father was devastated. Tanya's sister ended up in jail within the year. But her younger brother turned to the Lord.

Tanya and her boyfriend took sides, however. Tanya sided with her mother; her boyfriend sided with her father. As a result their relationship fizzled, right along with their faith. Tanya quit college and drifted from one bad relationship to the next, searching for the love and security she craved.

Five years later, Tanya was trying on relationships as if they were clothes—looking for a fit and finding only heartache. She was continuing her downward spiral as she left God behind.

Satan had pulled Tanya down when she was at her strongest. She was like Rehoboam, who plummeted after his kingdom was firmly established. Paul warns us to be on our guard: "If you think you are standing firm, be careful that you don't fall!" (1 Cor. 10:12).

Some of my biggest defeats in homeschooling have come when things were going well, after I was established and strong.

When I began to rely on my own wisdom, scheduling, and creativity, I suddenly found myself slipping into a downward spiral. As the downward spiral continued, I knew I needed to seek God with renewed fervency. Paul said, "When I am weak, then I am strong" (2 Cor. 12:10). How true!

It's a blessing to know I cannot succeed unless God carries me. Homeschooling keeps me on my knees. Every time I try to stand tall with pride, I'm brought to my knees because of my need for the Lord. Firmly, I've set my heart on seeking the Lord—now and always.

Lord, it appears the first step toward evil is the sin of pride. Make me realize every day that I am strong only because you make me that way. You are the rock upon which our school is built. You are the sure Foundation. Stop me before I even start toward the edge, and redirect my heart toward your will. Hold me to that promise, Lord. Amen.

25

Soul Food

"Why spend money on what is not bread, and your labor on what does not satisfy? Listen, listen to me, and eat what is good, and your soul will delight in the richest of fare." (Isa. 55:2)

I battled bulimia for six years and, ultimately, overcame. As a result, I have a great interest in reading books and articles on addictive behaviors and the many ways people attempt to fill the hunger in their lives. My heart aches for others who also struggle with addictions. I've been there. I know the feeling, all too well, of consuming but never being satisfied.

Here's an excerpt from an article I wrote about my experience in *Women Alive* called, "When Food Was My Master":

> When my parents moved across town the summer before my senior year of high school, I didn't think it would be a problem. But I began a pattern of "coping" that year that turned into a nightmare. At the new school, I was afraid to make friends. I was lonely and insecure. I felt like I had no one to turn to. I was a Christian, but I felt far from God. I ate to fill the void, then worked it off in weight-training class and started over again.
>
> Food was the first thing I thought about when I woke up and the last thing I thought about at night. I had tried everything I knew to break my addiction, but nothing worked for long. Even the horrible guilt I felt didn't stop me.[12]

For six long years I was in a vicious cycle of bingeing, purging, guilt, and repentance. Food was a cruel master. Its death grip on me wasn't released until I saw it for what it was—a false god. Only when I cried out to the Master of Love was I rescued by grace. And every time I fell, he picked me up, dusted me off, and set me on the right path once again.

I discovered the same truth Drs. Hemfelt, Minirth, and Meier discuss in their book, *We Are Driven*:

> Recognizing a false god for what it is—an addiction—is an important step toward recovering from its control.

Removing the addiction is the obvious next step, but filling the gap that is left by the addiction may be the most important step of all. If a healthy replacement for the addiction isn't found to fill the recovering person's deepest needs, the former addict often slips back into the old compulsion or picks up a new one.[13]

Food addicts can recover, only to find new addictions—shopping, work, alcohol, gambling, or sex—you name it. As long as the hunger remains unsatisfied, they merely slide from one addiction to another. Unless God is given first place in their lives, worldly addictions will be all they have.

As parent educators we have a solemn duty to feed our children food that satisfies them. Spending time reading the Bible illustrates just how important we believe it is to feed on God's Word. Children often learn by example and what they see filling us is what they'll be inclined to feed on as well.

What will you feed your children today?

O, Lord of my desires, you've filled me with the rich, satisfying taste of your Word. It gives me strength to accomplish great things in your name. I never tire from eating at your table. You alone bring lasting contentment. Thank you for feeding me from the feast of your Word. Amen.

26

Crossroads

This is what the LORD says: "Stand at the crossroads and look; ask for the ancient paths, ask where the good way is, and walk in it, and you will find rest for your souls. But you said, 'We will not walk in it.'

I appointed watchmen over you and said, 'Listen to the sound of the trumpet!' But you said, 'We will not listen.' (Jer. 6:16, 17)

One of my journal entries in 1999 reflects my thoughts on the verses above:

"This [passage] applies to every crossroad of life, the big and the small. I must be still and truly look at the options. What is the ancient path (the proven, the true, the established)? It may not be the path I would choose and it won't be the one everybody else is traveling on."

In marriage, family, friendships, conversations, movie and book choices, clothing, shopping habits, and eating—there is a God Way. Even if I have no human companion I will find rest there. My soul will be at peace. In the end it will bring me true and lasting happiness.

How difficult is it to determine the Ancient Path from the Path of Least Resistance? God's Way or the World's Super Highway? There are four tests I apply before deciding.

First, I look at my guidebook—the Bible. I want to see what light it sheds on my problems and questions. The Bible contains the truth of God's character, personality, and love for us. It holds the record of God's dealings with his people—a record for us to use when deciding the direction our own lives should take. History is a great learning tool for us to observe those individuals that lived upright lives and those who did not.

Oftentimes a crossroad turns out to be just a detour the enemy places before us, hoping to divert us from our true course. Wycliffe missionary Joanne Shetler tells about a crossroad that some recent Filipino converts encountered. Being new Christians, they asked if chewing betel nut (a customary practice in their village) should stop?

"I sent them back to Scripture," she said. "See what you can find about it in the Bible." They couldn't find anything.

"Is there anything about gossip in the Bible?" Joanne asked. There was plenty.

"Since that was a much bigger problem in Balangao than betel nut chewing, I [Joanne] suggested, 'Maybe we should just work on what is clearly forbidden first, then we can go to the betel nut.' They still haven't gotten to betel nut chewing."[14]

Second, I enter into prayer. I put forth all my questions and possible options before the Lord. I'm not unlike King Jehoshaphat, who before facing the armies of Moab and Ammon threatening to destroy Jerusalem, prayed to God (see 2 Chron. 20). The king knew that he and his people were helpless, and openly admitted their rescue could come only from God. He pleaded with the Lord on behalf of Israel, and God gave his reply in 2 Chronicles 20:15-17. When they obeyed God's instructions, he gave them the victory against their enemies.

Third, I seek godly counsel from other believers. My husband, my parents, and my sisters are the believers I turn to frequently for Christian counsel. They all spend time in the Word and in prayer. They're close to me, personally, and strive to counsel me from a biblical standpoint. They want only God's best for me, and I trust their godly wisdom.

Finally, I use my own judgment. I do this in conjunction with the first three: the Bible, prayer, and godly counsel. Our God-given intellect is a wonderful attribute, but it's not infallible. Combining it with other godly resources is critical.

Two key words in today's Scripture are *ask* and *walk*—we must do both. Why bother to *ask* God for his view on our situation if we don't *walk* in the light of his advice? We might as well get back on that World's Super Highway and go along our merry way, mired in ignorance and disobedience.

Consider Jerusalem's response in verse 17: "We will not walk in it" . . . "We will not listen." I can almost see them screwing up their faces and stomping their feet like two-year-olds who've just learned to say "No!"

Why all this utter stubbornness? Their heavenly Father is telling them the very best way to proceed, yet they refuse it. We too have the same choice at every crossroad in our lives, including our homeschooling dilemmas. We can ask God: What curriculum should I use? How should I discipline my children? How can I present this concept in a way they can grasp? Should I take today off to recharge or work through this slump? He will tell us if we ask him. Then we also must be willing to honor him by obeying the answer we've asked for. If we do, he will give us rest for our souls.

Dear Lord, let me ask for your counsel and walk in it always. We both know how stubborn I can be. Grant me a humble heart and a listening ear. Use my life as an example to teach my children about handling the crossroads of life. Amen.

27

I Can Face Tomorrow

"I have told you these things, so that in me you may have peace. In this world you will have trouble. But take heart! I have overcome the world." (John 16:33)

During the Easter season the enemy works considerably harder to confuse and dishearten us, leaving us feeling abandoned and forsaken. Along with Christmas, Easter is a time we should anticipate with great joy. It's the holiday that reminds us of our Savior's victory over the grave and death—the reason for our eternal hope. Yet so often we get bogged down in the details of holiday activity and forget to actually celebrate.

Church plays and musicals can be wonderful rituals of worship and praise, or they can turn into an exhausting marathon filled with costume fittings, rehearsals, makeup sessions, and stage fright. Even our traditional customs of baking desserts, decorating eggs, and spending special family time together can work to keep us from enjoying the true message of Easter.

So how can we keep the devil from winning during the Easter season? Jesus says to take heart because he's "overcome the world" AND defeated the "prince of this world" (John 14:30). Stay focused on Jesus and the undying hope of the resurrection!

Bill Gaither's hymn *Because He Lives* states we can face tomorrow because our Savior lives! It doesn't matter what's happening or how busy we are. Peace is ours amid even the darkest of times, because Christ has overcome the world. Share that hope in your classroom as each Easter season approaches. Give your children specific examples of how God has given you hope for a bright and glorious future. Greet your children on Easter morning with, "He is risen," and let them respond, "He is risen, indeed!"

Lord Jesus, Easter is meant to celebrate the enormous hope of your resurrection. But often that hope rests beneath an Easter egg hunt. Our propensity for new clothes and chocolate candy eggs takes away from the spirit of the holiday as well. Help me keep my focus on you. Remind me that you're not on the cross. You are not in the tomb, but in heaven, having gained victory over sin and death. Because of this fact, I can now look forward to spending eternity with you. Make that my focus at home and in the classroom, dear Savior. Amen.

28

Benjamin's Blessing

About Benjamin he said: "Let the beloved of the LORD rest secure in him, for he shields him all day long, and the one the LORD loves rests between his shoulders." (Deut. 33:12)

We were in the middle of the Twenty-first Psalm during our morning devotions, when suddenly I was overwhelmed with the desire to bestow the blessings of that psalm on my girls. They knelt by the couch, a little bewildered, but anticipating something new. They closed their eyes, and I placed my hands on their heads and prayed through the psalm. I inserted each girl's name and personalized the words as I went. We finished with smiles and tears. Then together we prayed a blessing on their father, too. Afterward we called Jeff at work to tell him about his blessing. He said he would read the psalm as soon as he got off the phone. There are many blessing passages in the Bible. They're great prayer starters and encouraging motivators. Best of all, they paint powerful images of love and good will for others.

Benjamin's blessing from Deuteronomy 33 is rich with imagery. Jacob said, "Let the beloved of the LORD rest secure in him." What a message to give our kids! We can use this Scripture to say to them, "God loves you. You can lean back and rest in his arms because he's crazy about you."

Jacob told Benjamin that God shielded him all day long. That's another great message for our children. They need to know the enemy can sneak up on them. God is always watching to protect them from harm.

In the third line of this short but powerful blessing, Jacob said, "The one the LORD loves rests between his shoulders." What a place to be! Our children need to hear that they can rest on God's powerful shoulders. I want them to keep this image. They'll never grow too big for God to carry. They can rest upon him when they feel harassed and helpless.

Jacob blessed all twelve of his sons. Each blessing was as individual as the boy who received it. Use scripture as a framework for your blessings. You can choose passages that fit the personality, gifts, and interests of the child that you want to encourage. A blessing can challenge a child to rise to a new level, but it should never be used manipulatively to force a child into a mold of your own making.

God has a blessing for you to give each of your children. If you make a habit of speaking blessings to them, your children can be confident of your love and that God has a special plan for their lives.

Dear Lord, you know how important encouraging words are to each of us. Help me to pour out your blessings on my children this week. Help me find ways to speak reassurance and praise to them on a regular basis, so they'll know I love them. More important, show them you'll always be there for them. Amen.

(An excellent resource for blessing the people in your life is the book, *The Blessing*, by Gary Smalley and John Trent.)

29

What Do You Have?

The wife of a man from the company of the prophets cried out to Elisha, "Your servant my husband is dead, and you know that he revered the LORD. But now his creditor is coming to take my two boys as his slaves."

Elisha replied to her, "How can I help you? Tell me, what do you have in your house?"

"Your servant has nothing there at all," she said, "except a little oil." (2 Kings 4:1, 2)

The poor woman in this story didn't have much of a life going for her. Her husband was now dead, and all he'd left her with was a stack of unpaid bills. Creditors were threatening forced labor on her sons as a method of repayment.

She had nothing else left, or so she thought, with which to pay off her debt.

She pleaded with God's servant, Elisha, for advice on her situation. Elisha asked the widow how he could help. He also wanted to know what she had left in her house. The widow told him she only had a small amount of oil. How in the world could she and her sons benefit from that?

Elisha's question must have perplexed this woman, but he did not ask it without good reason—he wanted her to witness and participate in God's miraculous way of meeting her needs.

Elisha told the widow to get some jars, and not just a few. She and her sons set out the jars they had and all the jars they had borrowed from neighbors, and God filled them. (Notice how God included the neighbors in on this family's miracle as well.) Similarly, we might have to set out some *jars* of our own if we want God to work a miracle for us. He will fulfill our needs and he might even choose an unorthodox method to do it. God is famous for unconventional methods. We should be open to all possibilities.

Maybe we have financial concerns like the widow in this story. Or we may seek healing for a physical ailment, need relief from emotional distress, or desire restoration of a broken relationship. So, what are we waiting for? Let's line up those jars! Borrow more if needed!

Notice when the widow answered Elisha's question she referred to herself as "your servant." Her humble attitude was equally as important to God as her willingness to borrow more jars. She did not preface her request with an attitude of deservedness. She didn't demand help from Elijah. She was desperate and thankful for anything she could get. The widow displayed a faith-filled character and genuine reverence.

I'm certain God wants us to be like this widow in our approach to homeschooling too. First, we must recognize our need for his help. Second, he'll want to know what's in us that he can use. Finally, by faith, we will need to set out our jars, and watch him fill our homeschool with abundant blessings. And whatever our homeschooling debt is, he will more than meet it.

What a wonderful God we serve!

Lord God, I don't always have the faith to believe you can multiply what I have to meet my needs. I do have a little knowledge, a little patience, a little enthusiasm, and a little love. I want to make them available to you in reverent humility. I give them to you now. Pour your blessings into our school this week. Help me believe you'll meet all our other needs as well. Amen.

30

Overtaken by Gladness and Joy

And a highway will be there; it will be called the Way of Holiness. The unclean will not journey on it; it will be for those who walk in that Way; wicked fools will not go about on it. . . . But only the redeemed will walk there, and the ransomed of the LORD will return. They will enter Zion with singing; everlasting joy will crown their heads. Gladness and joy will overtake them, and sorrow and sighing will flee away. (Isa. 35:8–10)

How many times do circumstances beyond our control overtake us: We face a serious illness or death, the loss of a job, or the breakup of a marriage? On the other hand, how many times do we also experience periods of joy, happiness, and peace, such as the birth of a child, a lovely wedding, or an anniversary celebration? Anything in life can serve to overtake us in some profound manner, and as long as we live, we will have instances that bring us sorrow and gladness.

God promises one day, however, that "the redeemed" will know only "gladness and joy" and that "sorrow and sighing will flee." When I read these verses, I picture Mr. Gladness and Ms. Joy cruising down Interstate Holiness in a snazzy new sports car, looking for any signs of the So Sad Twins—Sorrow and Suffering. Can't you just see them now, stopping here and there to offer hope and to clean up messes left behind by the evil Sorrow and Suffering? Maybe those nasty twins have sideswiped you and left you reeling in the Ditch of Despair. Never fear, Gladness and Joy are here! They tow your smashed faith right out of that ditch, help you make repairs, and soon have you humming along the Interstate of Holiness once again.

Gladness and Joy want us involved in their cool act of encouraging others. Several years ago my mom planned a birthday trip to the beach for my dad. Before my folks headed to the beach, my mom suggested they stop for breakfast in town. Imagine my dad's surprise when the rest of the family was gathered inside the restaurant. He was overtaken with joy—speechless, in fact.

God wants to fill our lives and our schoolrooms with his abundant gladness and joy. Share this devotion with your children today and discuss ways your family has been overtaken by Gladness and Joy. Perhaps you can also plan some activities to lend them a hand in their relentless job of smashing the Sorrow and Suffering Twins! Now, wouldn't that be fun?

Lord, thank you for sending Gladness and Joy to look out for me as I drive along your highway. I've been pushed into the Ditch of Despair many times by Sorrow and Suffering, but Gladness and Joy have always towed me out of it and kept me going. I can't wait for the day when those horrible Sorrow and Suffering Twins, and all their other foul relations, are history! Amen.

31

None Excluded

Let no foreigner who has bound himself to the LORD say, "The LORD will surely exclude me from his people." And let not any eunuch complain, "I am only a dry tree. . . ."

"For my house will be called a house of prayer for all nations." The Sovereign LORD declares—he who gathers the exiles of Israel: "I will gather still others to them beside those already gathered." (Isa. 56:3, 7, 8)

One evening, following a wonderful dinner with friends, Jeff and I took a tour of Rick and Alice's orchard. We learned tons about fruit trees that evening. In our jaunt I noticed some of the tree branches were tied off with strips of cloth. They looked like wounded soldiers wrapped up in bandages.

"What happened?" I asked. "Did the limbs break off in a storm?"

Alice explained that Rick was in the process of grafting limbs of different varieties onto these older, established trees.

"People want the latest kind of cherry faster than we can grow new stock," she said. "Rather than change plantings all the time, we can graft branches onto existing trees and they'll produce fruit more quickly."

Pointing to the tree on our right, she said, "This one is more resistant to standing water and makes a good base for the Sweetheart variety, a good eating cherry that doesn't grow well in our wet climate."

Doesn't this sound like God's plan for the world's people? By way of Christ, he has grafted non-Jewish folks into his family tree (see Rom. 11:17–23). Even if we weren't born Jewish we can still be called his chosen people, by being grafted into the family tree. Of course, the end result is that we will produce luscious, spiritual fruit.

Perhaps you've had a difficult life and do not have a background rooted in Christianity. It doesn't matter where you were born, what your background is, or what you've done— God can graft you into his family. No one is excluded from his invitation.

Foreigner is a word that does not exist in the house of the Lord. We don't have to become religious before we can welcome his offer. All we need do is accept it. What the world sees as broken and wounded people, God sees as potential, fruitful inhabitants for the Kingdom—just waiting to be drafted or grafted into the family.

Dear God, I'm so glad to be called and chosen by you, part of a holy nation! Thank you for grafting me into the family tree and letting me partake of your bountiful blessings. Give me opportunities to tell others that this offer applies to them, as well. May our family be witnesses of, and to, your love. Incorporate this into our school, Lord, and remind us always of the blessings that come with being included in your family. Amen.

32

Holding My Tongue

Aaron's sons Nadab and Abihu took their censers, put fire in them and added incense; and they offered unauthorized fire before the LORD, contrary to his command. So fire came out from the presence of the LORD and consumed them, and they died before the LORD. Moses then said to Aaron, "This is what the LORD spoke of when he said: 'Among those who approach me I will show myself holy; in the sight of all the people I will be honored.'" Aaron remained silent.
(Lev. 10:1–3)

Remaining silent has never been my strong suit. My Bible is filled with underlined passages and marginal notes on this very subject, precisely because of my weakness in this area. That's why this verse about Aaron and his sons presents a special challenge to me.

Aaron's sons disobeyed a direct command from God. Their punishment was instantaneous and extreme; God showed the Israelites he meant business. Yet Aaron said nothing. He made no excuse for his sons, nor did he question God's judgment upon them. His was an articulate silence.

As a mother my first instinct is to protect my girls from the consequences of pain and humiliation—I don't want them to suffer. But if they knowingly sin, as did Aaron's sons, then I must proceed with caution. If I jump in and try to fix things, I could be running roughshod over vital lessons God wants them to learn. It takes spiritual discernment to know when to help and when to keep silent.

In order to determine my actions, I ask myself these four questions:

1. Did my child know the difference between right and wrong in this instance?
2. Have I equipped, motivated, and encouraged her to obey?
3. Am I modeling obedience for her?
4. Have I applied discipline fairly and consistently?

If I've been faithful in all these things, then it may be God's turn to speak.

His voice will be difficult for my children to hear if I'm continually offering up my opinion with "I told you so's" and "you should have's." The most effective course of action I can take now is to pray for them, listen to them, and reassure them I love them in spite of what's happened.

No sooner had I written these words, than a scenario presented itself—giving me the perfect opportunity to test both Launa and myself. Launa had a project to write a research report for school. We spent one week preparing for it together. We outlined the steps, looked over examples, and made a trip to the library for additional resources. I then wrote out step-by-step assignments that would assist her as she tackled the thousand-word report.

After the preparation week, she had one week to read and take notes. By the following Monday, she should have been ready to begin her rough draft. Throughout that week, Launa assured me she was reading the material and making her notes. However, when Monday morning finally rolled around, Launa presented me with her work. I could see right away the material she had written wouldn't be enough to cover a thousand words—maybe three hundred, at most. The rest of her notes had mysteriously disappeared. She had no other choice but to continue reading and taking notes in her spare time in order to arrive where she was supposed to be.

I was tempted to allow her to cut corners and slide on some of the work. That would certainly have made the week easier for both of us, but doing that would have only reinforced reward for unacceptable work. Instead, Jeff and I suspended her extra activities for one week until the work was finished. I encouraged her and explained my reasons for not allowing her extra time during class sessions to complete the assignment. The entire family felt the consequences of disobedience as Launa struggled to complete the assignment.

It's extremely difficult not to nag and scold whenever one of my children finds themselves in a pit of their own making. I hate to see them so miserable, but I also resent the extra burden they've placed on me. I really would rather have the whole mess behind me, but I know this is a learning and teaching time. Instead, I hold my tongue while God teaches them a lesson in responsibility. My job is to hold them tightly with a loving, firm embrace.

Lord, disciplining my children is not easy! Thank you for showing me that silence can be a much more effective way to reach them than yelling or berating them. Continue to check my spirit when it's time for me to step back and let you do your work in them. Give me ways in which I can continually motivate and reward them for obedience. Help me to always discipline them fairly. And, most of all, thank you for loving them even more than I do. Amen.

33

Showing the Way

He who heeds discipline shows the way to life, but whoever ignores correction leads others astray. (Prov. 10:17)

Our unsettling journey began with a letter sent anonymously from someone in our Sunday school class. They criticized Jeff and me as leaders of the class and denigrated us as individuals. The writer even went so far as to suggest the entire class felt this way and ended by saying we would be better off leaving the class and the church.

Needless to say, Jeff and I reeled with pain and shock. What could we possibly have done to elicit such a forceful attack? We prayed about it, committed it to God, then ripped it out of his hands, and fumed over it some more. Finally, we met with our Sunday school teacher and prayed about it together. We decided the best course of action was to be open and honest. On the following Sunday we stood and apologized to our class for anything we'd done to fail them as leaders, friends, and fellow believers. We spoke of the letter and about what the Bible says to do when we have a problem with a brother (see Matt. 18:15–17). We also told them it would have been far less painful for one of them to approach us directly.

We could have chosen to ignore the letter, and console ourselves that we were targets of someone's vindictiveness. Several people told us that was the best option for dealing with unsigned letters. But when we put it before God, we felt him leading us to openly acknowledge our imperfections. Through it all, our girls quietly watched our response. It was humbling. We stumbled many times along the way, but I believe we modeled godly obedience during this trial.

If Jeff and I had continued to react with hurt and resentment, we would have been as guilty as the person who wrote the letter. Our choice was to exemplify Christ's attitude of forgiveness over and over again. Because we obeyed, God used the letter to benefit not only us, but also our family. We hope the members of our Sunday school class, including the letter writer, also benefited. Throughout the ordeal we were keenly aware of what Jesus must have felt during his own betrayal.

The attitude we display while under God's discipline will most likely be the attitude our children will take when we correct them. If we show a humble heart and a willingness to ask for forgiveness, instead of stiff-necked resistance, we'll leave a lasting impression that words alone could never communicate. It's a difficult lesson, but an invaluable one.

Dear God, you know I hate to be disciplined. I hated it as a child and still do today. But you've reminded me once again of the good that comes from undergoing your correction. Help me submit willingly to your wisdom. Allow me to be a godly model in front of my children, so that when they are disciplined they will respond accordingly. Amen.

34

Waiting, We Walk

Yes, LORD, walking in the way of your laws, we wait for you; your name and renown are the desire of our hearts. (Isa. 26:8)

Today's modern woman seems to be able to do it all: juggle housework, run errands, raise children, and even tackle homeschooling. We are a veritable whirlwind of nonstop activity, but ask us to *wait* and we are nonplussed.

Wait? Why? What for?

Waiting doesn't accomplish anything, or so we think. Especially difficult are those times God asks us to wait. However, God uses periods of waiting to achieve dramatic results in his people.

Our lives are full of places we must stop and wait: a busy doctor's office, a congested highway, or the Internet (for those of us with barbarically slow dial-up connections). Even so, we still find things to occupy ourselves during these times, too. We read a magazine while waiting on the doctor. We pop in a tape or CD to listen to while stuck in traffic. We make out a grocery list while we're waiting to surf the internet, but what can we do while we're waiting on God? Good question!

Isaiah says we should walk, not just anywhere, but in the way of God's laws. While waiting for a response from God in any situation, we can follow the example of the apostles in Acts 1:15–26—praying, seeking God's guidance, and getting organized. Waiting for God to work doesn't mean sitting around doing nothing. We must do what we can—while we can—as long as we don't run ahead of God.

So, "Don't be impatient for the Lord to act! Keep traveling steadily along his pathway and in due season he will honor you with every blessing" (Ps. 37:34, TLB). Keep traveling. Move steadily. You may not have all the answers right now, but you know what to do until you get them.

What are you waiting for?

- A son or daughter to choose Christ?
- A light of understanding in your child's eyes after explaining a particularly difficult math problem?
- The healing of a loved one?
- Your financial situation to improve?

Don't stop walking in God's ways while you're awaiting an answer. It may feel like an eternity, but it won't be. Remember that faith is expectant, always expectant.

Lord Jesus, it feels like forever since you asked me to wait. Can you give me any hint or clue as to your response—anything but silence? I'm used to keeping busy, Lord, and I'm uncomfortable with inactivity. Show me what I can do while waiting on you. Keep me walking in your laws, and use this period of waiting for my edification and your glory. Amen.

35

Godly Sorrow Brings Repentance

Now I am happy, not because you were made sorry, but because your sorrow led you to repentance. For you became sorrowful as God intended . . . Godly sorrow brings repentance that leads to salvation and leaves no regret, but worldly sorrow brings death. (2 Cor. 7: 9, 10)

Our girls had a big fight one evening just before bedtime. Fatigue is probably the reason it got out of hand in the first place. One girl said she was sorry, but the other refused to apologize.

They ended up in our bedroom rehashing it for more than another hour.

Jeff and I were at a loss as to how to resolve the conflict. For lack of a better idea, we decided to separate into pairs, each parent with a child. As we discussed the girl's fight, it became apparent that a spiritual battle was taking place inside of them.

Finally, after much discussion, the girls began to realize that this fight was much more than sister against sister—it was a battle for their "spirits." With no prompting from us, the girls forgave each other and made amends for their behavior. After a long two hours, we all collapsed into bed and slept great.

Unfortunately, the girls aren't the only ones in our home in need of forgiveness. One day during our morning prayer time together, I allowed myself to get a little carried away. A couple we knew was having marital problems. I revealed more information than I should have in front of the girls.

Tara gently interrupted. "But, Mom, isn't that gossip?"

Right then, I had a choice to make. I didn't want to admit I was wrong, and yet my role as a godly example had been compromised. Instantly, my pride reared its ugly head, but at the same time the Holy Spirit convicted me with humility. My choice was made.

"Yes, Tara," I said, "you're right, that was gossip. You didn't need to know all those details. I'm sorry. Please forgive me."

God often works through my husband and my children to correct me. My behavior in front of the girls will set the tone for how they act and react when their own behavior is corrected. If I model a godly example before them, they will learn to hear the Lord's voice and respond accordingly.

In Paul's first letter to the Corinthian believers, his painful words brought godly sorrow, repentance, and healing within that church. Our role as teachers is much more than academic. Like Paul with the Corinthians, our job as homeschoolers is to nurture the spiritual conscience of each child in our charge, teaching and modeling for them a spirit that won't grieve God.

Lord, remind me how important godly sorrow is when confronted with a problem with one of our children. Don't let me be satisfied with a quick fix or a patch-up job. Help me press on to a resolution even when I am tired, frustrated, or embarrassed. Bestow upon me wisdom and discernment in leading my children to prayer and repentance. I know you will do the same when I sin, Lord. Amen.

36

What Does God Want?

And now . . . what does the LORD your God ask of you but to fear the LORD your God, to walk in all his ways, to love him, to serve the LORD your God with all your heart and with all your soul, and to observe the LORD's commands and decrees that I am giving you today for your own good? (Deut. 10:12, 13)

Throughout our lives one question seems to take priority: "What do you want?" We look for the answer to this all-important question in every relationship we have. Pleasing others, especially those closest to us, is a primary goal.

This desire to please others remains at the forefront of our lives. We try our hardest to be liked. This is one of the reasons teens so often get into trouble. Their consciences say no, but their friends say yes. Because teens want to be accepted and liked by their peers they get involved in activities that are clearly wrong.

But the desire to please doesn't stop at adolescent age. When it's time to enter the working world, it follows right along. We ask our boss, "What do you want?" We have such a strong drive for acceptance.

My first "real" job (baby-sitting and berry picking don't count), was at the local A&W Restaurant. My boss's motto was, "Always look busy, " and he liked me because I found ways to do just that. I knew what he wanted. If there were no customers to serve, I wiped counters, washed dishes, and cleaned the windows or the bathrooms. We got along famously!

As I grew older this desire to please others remained right with me. I tried to read body language. I attempted to create a harmonious and happy environment wherever I found myself. When carried to the extreme, however, this behavior of trying to please everyone is not healthy.

Truth be told, there is measure of selfishness in asking the question, "What do you want?" Do we try to please the boss so we can reap a pay raise or promotion? Do we selfishly ask our spouse, "What can I do for you?" in hopes of gleaning some sort of compensation? And yet as Christians we respond the majority of the time out of love and kindness when we ask the question, "What do you want?"

God knows our nature and sets his expectations of us up front. After committing our life to the Lord, we begin asking that same question: "What do you want, Lord? What do you expect from me, God? How can I please you?" He tells us in Deuteronomy 10:

- We are to "fear" him, having reverence and awe for his character.
- We are to "walk in all his ways," loving him and serving him with our total being.
- We are to keep his commands, knowing they are there to keep us healthy, happy, and peaceful.

The *Westminster Shorter Catechism* puts it like this:

"Q—What is the chief end of man?"

"A—Man's chief end is to glorify God and to enjoy him forever."[15]

Author Charles Swindoll agrees: "Our sole purpose, our basic reason for existence, is to bring maximum glory to our God. Scripture virtually pulsates with the mandate, 'Glorify God!'"[16]

God wants us to love him for himself—not because of potential reward or punishment. He wants us to grow past the pleasing stage and obey him out of love.

Lord, thank you for telling us what pleases you. And thank you for letting us know you only want it done from a heart of love, not because we are forced to. Show me ways I can teach my children your expectations, and that they come from a loving Father, one who has only their best interests at heart. Amen.

37

The Law Was God's Idea

*These are the commands, decrees and laws the LORD your God directed me to teach you to observe . . . **so that** you, your children and their children after them may fear the LORD your God as long as you live by keeping all his decrees and commands that I give you, and **so that** you may enjoy long life. . . . and be careful to obey **so that** it may go well with you and that you may increase greatly . . . just as the LORD, the God of your fathers, promised you. (Deut. 6:1–3, author's emphasis)*

The Ten Commandments came straight from the hand of God. Moses was simply the delivering servant. It's important we teach our kids that these are God's commandments—not man-made rules—and are to be passed down from one generation to the next.

My parents taught me from God's Word as did their parents before them. Now it's time for me to pass the teaching on to a new generation. This teaching includes warning them of the consequences of sin.

Dr. James Dobson relates the story of how his mother taught him the importance of fearing God. One evening after reading the biblical account of Samson's life, she solemnly told him,

> "There are terrible consequences to sin. Even if you repent and are forgiven, you will still suffer for breaking the laws of God. They are there to protect you. If you defy them, you will pay the price for your disobedience." Then she talked to me about gravity, one of God's physical laws. You must also know that God's *moral* laws are just as real as his physical laws. You can't break them without crashing sooner or later.[17]

Our holy, perfect God gave us rules to live by. They aren't for his benefit; they are for our benefit. Deuteronomy 6 gives three reasons why obeying God is a win-win situation. I refer to them as the "so thats." God uses these "so thats" in response to the ever-present question, "Why should I obey?"

In the first example, Moses tells the Israelites (this applies to us, too) to observe God's commands, decrees, and laws "*so that* [they], [their] children, and [their] grandchildren may fear . . . God as long as [they] live." The choices we make don't just affect us, but they affect future generations as well. Children need to learn there are consequences to every action (be it good or bad) that can filter down to subsequent generations.

Next, we see Moses directing the people to, "[Keep] his decrees and commands . . . *so that* you may enjoy long life." One would only want a long life if it were full and satisfying, not difficult and perilous. God knows this and has instructed us accordingly.

Finally, we read, "be careful to obey *so that* it may go well with you and that you may increase greatly." Obedience to God will attract unbelievers to him and cause the kingdom of God to multiply. Cheerful, willing obedience is contagious, especially when the benefits of following God's ways are reflected in us—joyful faces, peaceful homes, and unshakable faith during even the toughest times.

To coin a phrase, things just go better with God. When we fear him, love him, and obey his laws, our lives will be richer, fuller, and happier. Yes, the law was indeed God's idea because he loves us so much.

Dear Lord, you love us enough to give us commands to live by and to pass on to our children. You've also been gracious enough to explain why we should obey them. Help me embrace your "so thats" and infuse my children with a desire for an obedient spirit as well. We know there are benefits for obeying and consequences for disobeying. Keep us on the "obeying side," Lord. Amen.

38

The Same God

He who forms the mountains, creates the wind, and reveals his thoughts to man, he who turns dawn to darkness, and treads the high places of the earth—the LORD God Almighty is his name. (Amos 4:13)

My husband, Jeff, is a man of few words, so I can't always tell what he's thinking. I love it when he confides in me. I love to hear about his dreams and his concerns, and I feel honored, trusted, and important when he shares his innermost thoughts with me. It goes both ways. He is also my confidant and that has created a special bond between us.

Amos relates to us that God is our confidant, and he beautifully surrounds that statement with a description of God's divine abilities.

- His hands formed the mountains.
- He tells the wind where and when to blow.
- He commands the day to become night.
- He treads the high places of the earth.
- His name is Almighty.

Placed carefully in the center of the descriptions of God's divine capabilities are these words from Amos: God "reveals his thoughts to man."

This same God, who commands all of nature, also delights in revealing himself to us. Since the beginning of creation, when God walked and talked with Adam and Eve in the Garden of Eden, his priority has been to make himself known to humanity. Even after sin entered the world, God still communed with those who wanted to know him. He formed relationships with many: He walked with Enoch; he confided in Noah; he blessed Abraham; he fed Elijah; he rescued Daniel; and of course, he dealt with David, Solomon, Peter, John, and Paul. Patriarchs, prophets, kings, disciples, apostles—and now God wants to confide in us.

He desires to share the mystery of himself. Several verses confirm this truth:

- "He reveals the deep things of darkness and brings deep shadows into the light" (Job 12:22).
- "The LORD confides in those who fear him; he makes his covenant known to them" (Ps. 25:14).

- "The LORD detests a perverse man but takes the upright into his confidence" (Prov. 3:32).
- "He reveals deep and hidden things; he knows what lies in darkness, and light dwells with him" (Dan. 2:22).

Isn't it awesome our Creator chooses to share himself with his creation? And, after studying God's power and the intricacy of his works in science with our kids, we see how worthy God is of our praise. The closer we come to him, the more he'll confide in us. So, let's run eagerly to meet him and learn directly from the Divine Teacher.

Dear God, we've shared so many secrets over the years, and I take such great delight in each one. How wonderful it is to have you as my confidant! Although I can't hear you speak to me, I still feel your presence as you whisper to my soul. Allow my children to know you like this, too, sharing an ever-deepening love between Creator and child. Amen.

39

Contentment

I have learned to be content whatever the circumstances. I know what it is to be in need, and I know what it is to have plenty. I have learned the secret of being content in any and every situation, whether well fed or hungry, whether living in plenty or in want.
(Phil. 4:11, 12)

The first home Jeff and I owned was only seven hundred square feet. To my decorator eye it held limitless remodeling possibilities. It was located in a wonderful neighborhood within walking distance of a park, a library, and an upscale drug store—the kind with a specialty gift shop. We were thrilled. And best of all, it was ours.

Soon, though, warm weather gave way to cold, and what had been charming during the summer became confining during the dreary winter months. We had only one vehicle and Jeff used it for work. If I needed to go somewhere I walked. Trudging through the rain with a two-year-old was a hardship, so Tara and I stayed indoors unless it was absolutely necessary to get out. The heater struggled to keep the house warm, but never quite succeeded.

My cold and claustrophobic surroundings put a damper on my remodeling plans. I started to despise our bedroom with its orange and tan wallpaper, blue and white linoleum, and just enough space on either side of the bed to squeeze in and out. Our little fixer-upper wasn't so thrilling anymore.

By the following February we had made very little progress in our remodeling. Our new master bedroom and bath were framed in, but still needed lots of work. I was tired of mismatched rooms and skeletal walls. I wanted comfort. Bathing every morning in icy water did nothing to inspire a happy me, especially since I was pregnant again. During that long winter of my severe discontent, the Lord led me through a Bible study on—you guessed it—contentment.

Back then I had no idea I'd be joining the ranks of homeschooling moms, but God did. He saw me through that difficult year by changing me, not my circumstances. I've gone back over that study on contentment many times during my years of homeschooling the girls and have gained a new and better perspective each time.

Luci Swindoll writes about contentment in *Joy Breaks:*

The key to contentment is *to consider*. Consider who you are and be satisfied with that. Consider what you have and be satisfied with that. Consider what God's doing and be satisfied with that. You will be amazed at how much more comfortable you'll feel with yourself.[18]

Leroy Brownlow echoes that with, "Contentment consists not in multiplying our wealth, but decreasing our wants." . . . "We do not need very much and we do not need that very long."[19]

Homeschooling can be rife with opportunities for discontentment. We do sacrifice some to make our children's education a priority. At first the idea of teaching at home sounds charming—just like our fixer-upper. All sorts of lovely ideas start rolling around in our heads as we dream of character building and "remodeling" the condition of our kids' education. But soon winter comes and reality hits.

This is the time we need to cling to God as the source of our contentment. His presence alone is key to feeling satisfied no matter what. Whether or not we have a new home, a wonderful, functional classroom, or a good teaching-day experience—he leaves us with peace about it all.

Lord, this world is famous for breeding discontent. The world says I deserve the best, my happiness is paramount, and anything that gets in my way should be pushed aside. I know better, though—I know the secret to contentment lies with you. Continue to hold me fast when the walls feel as if they're closing in on me. Let me share this secret with other moms, as well. Amen.

40

Cause for Error

Jesus replied, "You are in error because you do not know the Scriptures or the power of God." (Matt. 22:29)

My birthday was rolling around, so Jeff and Tara took off one afternoon to shop for a present. In a store that specialized in kitchen products, Tara noticed a funny little gadget with a few garlic cloves lying beside it. "Yum, roasted garlic!" Being a true garlic lover, she couldn't help but pop a sample in her mouth. Boy, were her taste buds in for a big surprise!

Turns out the garlic cloves weren't roasted after all. They were raw. The salesclerk had peeled the garlic to demonstrate how that funny little gadget—the garlic peeler—worked. When the clerk saw Tara's eyes widen in shock, she rushed over with a box of mints hoping to quench the raging fire inside Tara's mouth. Tara committed a huge error. She didn't know the garlic was raw, and she had no idea raw garlic could be so powerful.

The Sadducees didn't receive amnesty for their ignorance either. They knew the Scripture all right, but they didn't know (understand) it. They read it and loved to quote from it, but they were clueless as to its power to change lives. Instead, they used Scripture to gain leverage over others. They approached Jesus in the guise of seekers, with the intent of catching him breaking a law. Naturally, Jesus wasn't fooled by their duplicity.

Every school year I build upon the knowledge my kids have gained from the previous year. When it comes to grammar I teach a few rules, and the girls use what they've learned. Then I teach a little more and, again, they use what I've taught them. Even with the lessons and practice the girls are still prone to making grammar mistakes. They know grammar, but they still don't know (understand) it.

The Sadducees in their arrogance thought they knew and understood the Scriptures. Wrong! True, they could quote verse after verse, but they totally missed the concept of the resurrection in the Scripture.

As homeschool moms, we may drill memory verses into the heads of our children. They may even excel at quoting Scripture. And their understanding of biblical information may confound even the most learned Bible professors. But if our children remain ignorant when it comes to applying Scriptures to their daily life, we have not done our job.

Remember, the raw, undiluted Word of God has the power to change our children's lives.

Dear Lord, prepare me to come before you, ready to hear your Holy Word. My children need to know who you really are. We live in a world ignorant of the truth and the power of your Word. It is the only source we have to truly overcome the strongholds of ignorance that surround us. Reveal your power in us and through us. Amen.

41

Practice What You Preach

Then Jesus said . . . "The teachers of the law and the Pharisees sit in Moses' seat. So you must obey them and do everything they tell you. But do not do what they do, for they do not practice what they preach." (Matt. 23:1–3)

I ran into an old friend recently. As we talked I discovered Harriet was pretty discouraged about her job. Perhaps you'll understand why when I tell you Harriet's last name: Homeschooler. 'Nuff said, right? Anyway, this is what she told me:

"The kids and I had such a hard year! September started off pretty well. I taught the children about discipline and dedicating their schoolwork to the Lord, but it wasn't long before the lessons got harder and they just seemed to give up. Then I got so busy with homeschooling, I ended up quitting the fitness program I started last summer and gained another ten pounds.

"November and December weren't any better. The kids and I studied about being thankful and about giving to others, and we even learned some new holiday songs, but do you think that did any good? No! My children are as ungrateful as ever! All they think about is themselves."

"How about the New Year?" I asked, hoping to hear something encouraging.

"Well, I thought maybe things would change after Christmas." Harriet sighed. "I taught a lesson on what it meant to be a new creation in Christ and how the Holy Spirit comes to live in us. But they haven't changed at all! I get so mad sometimes, I could just scream. In fact, I do scream. But, then again, I've always had a temper."

"Will your frustration keep you from participating in the Easter cantata?" I ventured. "I know how much all of you have always enjoyed being involved."

"Oh, Easter is another story! I talked till I was blue in the face about Christ's sacrifice on the cross, but do you think they cared about that? Oh no! They were completely caught up in the idea of an Easter egg hunt and candy.

"Then on Easter Sunday, after we'd already been at church for more than two hours, my husband and kids stood around visiting with the new family in our neighborhood. For Pete's sake, we can talk to them any time. They talked so long all the restaurants filled up. You guessed it; I had to go home and cook dinner.

"Finally, in May I took one last stab at homeschooling. I started my children on a Bible memorization program, but it just left them cold. No motivation whatsoever. They just don't seem interested in spiritual things. My daughter even challenged my authority by asking me why I didn't try memorizing along with them. I told her I've already memorized all I need to know. Besides, nothing sticks in my brain anymore."

Harriet sighed again and shook her head. "I just don't think I can homeschool again next year. It's a waste of time. The more I try to teach my children about God, the less they seem to understand. If only they'd follow my example . . ."

Lord, Harriet may not be a real person, but a lot of what she said hit home. I realize I'm not perfect, but allow my children to see in me a heart that's willing and compassionate before you. Make me an example of humility, obedience, and sincere repentance, a godly example my children can emulate and trust. Amen.

42

Making the Grade

"I tell you the truth," he said, "this poor widow has put in more than all the others. All these people gave their gifts out of their wealth; but she out of her poverty put in all she had to live on." (Luke 21:3, 4)

Several years ago on a long walk my dad and I had a special conversation. That dad-to-daughter conversation helped me become a better teacher. Dad spoke of the time he and Mom were in college. My dad has a doctorate in music education, and my mom has a master's degree in library science. Schoolwork, however, came much easier for my mom than it did for my dad.

"Whenever we had an assignment for a research paper, I'd start right away," my dad said. "I'd read voluminously, take notes, and slave over my paper—only to end up with a B. Your mother, however, would put it off till the last minute, throw something together the night before it was due, and get an A. It really bugged me back then, but I think I got more out of school than she did. I appreciate my education, because I really had to work hard for it."

I recalled his words recently when I read this quote from Buckminster Fuller:

> "If I ran a school, I'd give the average grade to the ones who gave me all the right answers, for being good parrots. I'd give the top grades to those who made a lot of mistakes and told me about them, and then told me what they learned from them."[20]

Many homeschool-educated kids do extremely well academically. When people learn that I homeschool my children, most respond enthusiastically. "I hear several of the recent national champions in spelling and geography were home-schooled children," they say. "In fact, I saw a kid on a game show the other night who . . ."

Those kids should certainly be applauded for their terrific accomplishments, but it's important to keep in mind that many kids don't even enter contests—much less win them. By the world's standards, they might not be "making the grade."

I think if Jesus were to visit the nation's homeschools, he'd be more impressed with traits such as generosity, obedience, honesty, or perseverance. He is more concerned with what's in the hearts than the grades on the paper. Yes, standards do matter, but it's more important for our kids to know that what they put into their work is what makes it valuable. They deserve our highest praise if they're doing their best and giving it their all, even if the final mark isn't an A.

Most families have a mix of kids; some children are academically inclined and some are academically challenged. Throughout his ministry Jesus met a mix of people, but he always found ways to uplift people who had less—less talent, less social status, less physical strength, and less money (just like the widow in the verses from Luke).

The poor widow's story challenges me to place more emphasis in my classroom on what matters to Jesus. He praised the widow because she gave all she had, even though she was poor. A child who struggles for two weeks to write an average paper but has fun learning in the process, deserves all our praise and encouragement. Jesus would give him an A+.

Lord, forgive me for the times I've measured my children strictly by their grades. Please help me see the areas in which they are doing well and those they need more help in. Most of all, I simply want to see them doing their best. Show me how to encourage them to enjoy the process of learning and to praise them when they work hard, regardless of the results. Amen.

43

Rule on Rule

Very well then, with foreign lips and strange tongues
God will speak to this people, to whom he said, "This is
the resting place, let the weary rest"; and, "This is the
place of repose"—but they would not listen. So then,
the word of the LORD to them will become:

> *Do and do, do and do,*
> *Rule on rule, rule on rule;*
> *A little here, a little there—*
> *so that they will go and fall backward,*
> *be injured and snared and captured.*
> (Isa. 28:11–13)

Why do we complicate Christianity when God
has made it so simple? Mary and Martha come

to mind. Martha and I are a lot alike. Just like her, I run around the house putting everything in order for visiting guests. Can't you just see Martha now?

"Hurry, Mary! We've got to sweep the floors, change the beds, bake the bread, and make the desserts (somehow, I think Martha would have made plenty of desserts). And we need fresh flowers in every room, don't you think so, Mary? Mary? Where is that girl?"

Mary is sitting with Jesus, listening to his teachings and enjoying his presence. That left Martha holding the rolling pin, so she decided to lay down a couple rules.

Rule #1—A good hostess stays in the kitchen until the meal is ready.

Rule #2—No one gets to visit with Jesus until everybody's fed and the dishes are done.

Martha turns to Jesus for a little moral support. After all, she is doing the work and Mary is sitting there acting as if she didn't have a care in the world. "Jesus, do something!" she said.

And he did. He said, "Martha, dear Martha, you're fussing far too much and getting yourself worked up over nothing. One thing only is essential, and Mary has chosen it—it's the main course, and won't be taken from her" (Luke 10:41, 42 *The Message*).

Jesus told Martha to take a break and focus on the most important thing—him. Martha and the people of Isaiah's time had much in common. They, too, were weary and needed a break, but would not listen when God invited them to come and rest. Instead, they kept busy with all the rules of their religion. God knew rules couldn't save his people. Their refusal to rest in his salvation only made them all the more anxious and vulnerable, especially to their enemies.

God is saying the very same to us today. "Come and find rest in me. Concentrate on what's truly important. Don't worry about all that other stuff." Our choice is simple: Either we sit at his feet and listen to the Living Word, or we hang out in the kitchen griping about all there is to do and having no help to do it.

What do we want our children to see—legalism or the freedom of sitting at Christ's feet? Every day brings challenges that might make us miss our spot before Jesus. So, like Mary, take those challenges and lay them at his feet. Jesus has a spot just for you.

Dearest Jesus, I want to sit at your feet like Mary, but I always end up back in the kitchen. Instill in me a desire to sit quietly before you and to bask in your presence. Place this same desire in the hearts of my children, and lead us all to rest in you. Amen.

44

What Do You Feed Your Mind?

Summing it all up, friends, I'd say you'll do best by fill-ing your minds and meditating on things true, noble, reputable, authentic, compelling, gracious—the best, not the worst; the beautiful, not the ugly; things to praise, not things to curse. Put into practice what you learned from me, what you heard and saw and real-ized. Do that, and God, who makes everything work together, will work you into his most excellent har-monies. (Phil. 4:8, 9 The Message)

Fifteen years ago I attended a revival in New York and heard the evangelist Stephen Manley preach. What he said that day changed my thinking about the words that come from my own mouth. Manley began his sermon by asking for a volunteer, and a teenage boy climbed onstage.

Then Manley poured water into a cup and held it at arm's length in front of the boy. "Okay, son," he said, "I want you to shake my arm." The boy did so, timidly at first, but with the evangelist's encouragement began to move it more forcefully. Water sloshed from side to side and splashed onto the platform at the front of the tent.

Manley thanked the boy whose part was done. The evangelist looked at us with penetrating eyes and asked, "Why did water spill from the cup?"

The crowd was silent at first, then finally someone said, "Because the boy shook your arm." That was an obvious answer, or so we thought. But Manley shook his head and repeated the question with more emphasis. "Why did water spill from the cup?"

We struggled to come up with the correct answer. A few more guesses were made, but they were all wrong. Finally, Manley answered his own question. It was profoundly simple: "Water spilled from the cup, because there was water inside the cup."

Our thought lives are like empty cups. If we don't continually allow the Holy Spirit to fill our minds and hearts, the muck and mire of the world will settle in and fill the cups of our souls. Then, whenever we're shaken, filth will rise and splash anyone close by. What spills out of the cup is what we permit to go in it. Allowing God to fill our minds with edifying thoughts will filter out the sediment of sin and constantly purify our hearts. Then when we get jostled, only the fruit of God's Spirit will pour out.

Our family started a new Christmas Eve tradition last year—giving a gift to Jesus. Each of us wrote out something we wanted Jesus to have. Then we folded up the papers and placed them on the tree. On Christmas morning, we unwrapped these gifts to Jesus and read aloud what we had written. I've kept mine in my Bible all year as a reminder of my gift to Jesus, and I look at it almost every day.

It says: "For your birthday this year, I give you my mouth for you to use to bless and encourage others."

I never imagined how much Jesus would give to me through a gift meant for him.

After my pastor preached a sermon on the tongue, I added to my paper, "Lord, tame my tongue." Then autumn came and I read Jesus' words in Matthew 12:34: "Out of the overflow [or abundance] of the heart the mouth speaks." At the bottom of my paper, I squeezed in, "Lord, change my heart."

This desire to have my mouth filled with blessing and encouragement is constantly tested in my schoolroom. With God's help, I can control what spills out of my mouth.

Dear Lord, I'm careful about what I allow of the world into my mind. However, my biggest problem is not with the world's filth, but with my own thought life. I find it difficult to concentrate on what's pure, noble, and praiseworthy and, instead, allow my thoughts to wander to criticism, complaining, and self-pity. Let your Spirit purify my heart and my thoughts, so that only Spirit-filled "water" will pour from me daily. Amen.

45

One God, One Devotion

Hear, O Israel: The LORD our God, the LORD is one. Love the LORD your God with all your heart and with all your soul and with all your strength. (Deut. 6:4, 5)

I feel like the juggler who keeps several plates turning at all times. Homeschool moms have to be pretty good jugglers, but one of the main reasons we work so hard to fulfill this teaching responsibility is that we love God.

But what if we didn't know which god to worship? Millions of people know there's something out there, some first cause, something bigger than they are, but they have no conception of a creator God. Author and speaker Ravi Zacharias tells how he discovered God in a land of polytheism:

> India is a land full of gods—330 million gods, to be exact. Searching for the one true God in that environment is almost laughable. I would say that the odds were 330-million-to-one that I should have found spiritual satisfaction in something other than Christianity. But I was hungry for *reality*. And *reality* is only found in Jesus.[21]

Do we teach our children that there's only one true God? Every day, we see eastern religions infiltrating our world—and not just in the school system. We see their influence in the magazines we read and the movies we watch. Even our churches are infected with the popular idea of honoring diversity.

Jesus was very clear on one point, a fact other religions neatly sidestep. He said, "I am the way and the truth and the life. No one comes to the Father except through me" (John 14:6). Worldly wisdom holds that Jesus was a prophet, a good man, but claims he got a little carried away when he stated that *he* was the *only* way to God.

Again, I quote from Ravi Zacharias:

> I once stood at the side of a road, watching the golden statue of a 'god' being transported from one temple to another. Thousands clamored to give an offering and to receive a blessing. The priests accompanying the god had incense and ash in their hands and generously distributed the deity's goodwill on any fruit or piece of clothing placed before them. . . . I asked a woman

who had just received her "blessing" if this god actually existed—or if he were just an expression of some inner hunger. She hesitated and then said, "If you think in your heart that he exists, then he does."

"What if you do not believe he exists?" I asked.

"Then he doesn't exist," she softly said.

God isn't merely whatever we hope "he" or "she" or "it" is. I think each of us wants to build life on more than a wish.[22]

As Christians, we have hope, but that's not all we have. We have proof that our God is the only true God. Through his birth, life, death, and resurrection, the God-man (Jesus) fulfilled more than 300 specific biblical prophecies regarding the Messiah. His miraculous power over space, time, nature, sickness, and death showed the power of God resting in Jesus. And today our own hearts testify that God is real.

Is this what we're teaching our children?

Dear Lord, many things once thought true have been challenged and proved false over the years. We know the world isn't flat. We know the universe doesn't revolve around the earth. And we know that the draining of bad blood doesn't make a person well. But we know that everything you ever said is true. Not one thing has been proved false. I praise you for your unchanging truth. Amen.

46

Thinning Out

"My father is the gardener. He cuts off every branch in me that bears no fruit, while every branch that does bear fruit he prunes so that it will be even more fruitful." (John 15:1, 2)

I love to garden, but I don't like thinning and pruning because it requires killing perfectly healthy plants. But I know if I don't make room for the plants while they're young, they'll die later for lack of breathing space. And if they don't die out, they'll mature into warped shapes that look more like science fiction characters than vegetables.

Spend some time this summer thinking about what to thin out of your schedule for next school year. If there's not enough "space" available for you and your children, then something in your schedule must be changed or thinned out. If that doesn't happen, some warped features may appear because there's not enough room for healthy growth.

You may have to eliminate some activities or bad habits. You may need to pull some programs or move out some activities to make room for new ones. There may even be an unhealthy friendship you or your child may need to let die. (This is a tough one, but sometimes drastic action must be taken.)

Be careful, though, because some weeds look like garden vegetables. I remember the day my dad showed me the difference between carrot sprouts and grass. Then he set me to work weeding the carrot row. I conscientiously pulled every last carrot in the row, leaving in its place a neatly growing line of grass. They looked so much alike.

When you begin to thin your garden of activities, even a music appreciation class may look like a healthy vegetable-sort-of-thing. Yet, if this class saps the time and energy from you that your children need, thin it out. The same is true for sports, additional computer training, ministry opportunities, and on and on. What looks like a carrot could be a weed; only your Father can show you the difference.

Don't be afraid to thin and prune. Learn from the past. And never forget your main goal—raising and teaching your children to be caring, loving, disciplined Christians.

Thinning Out

Dear Father, thank you for being the Master Gardener. Help me do some thinning this year, no matter how much I'd like to keep everything as it is. Give me your wisdom to know what to pull and what to let grow. I love you, Lord. Amen.

47

Break It Up

This is what the Lord says . . ."Break up your unplowed ground and do not sow among thorns." (Jer. 4:3)

Summer is a great time for reflecting on the past year and planning for the next. I take advantage of this lull in my hectic life to examine my heart. I look for any unplowed soil or thorns that could take root. Make "tilling the soil of your heart" and "getting rid of thorns" a priority, and do not let them choke your spiritual growth. Prepare your "soil" now for a healthy, productive school year to come.

Somehow, I had the idea that God was responsible for the plowing and sowing within our hearts. However, Jeremiah says that I am to "break up [my own] unplowed ground." I am responsible for helping make my heart ready to receive God's Word. It's impossible for a hardened heart to receive what God has to offer.

In the same way that I prepare myself, I must also encourage my children to "break up [the] unplowed ground" of their hearts. I use the summer time to study my kids and observe their behavior. How do they react to discipline, to hardship, to other family members, or to unexpected changes? What would make them more receptive to the Holy Spirit and to my teaching?

As homeschool moms and teachers, we must remember that God desires his land to be fruitful, not barren (see Ezek. 36:9, 10). He looks down hoping to see a harvest. We need to have that same vision for our children. We're partners with God in the work of the Kingdom. Preparing the ground for planting is our first concern.

But how do we soften hardened hearts?

First, plowing must be done in season (see Prov. 20:4). Farmers plow in the spring after rain has softened the ground, making it receptive to the plow and moist enough to nourish the seed. They plow under the stubble left after the last harvest, once again providing nourishment to the soil. But they don't till directly after sowing because the seeds need a chance to germinate undisturbed. And when it comes to our child's heart, we must do our plowing, sowing, and cultivating in the appropriate season.

Second, God says to let the land rest from time to time (see Exod. 34:21 and Isa. 28:24–26). We can't work the soil all year round. Give your kids a break from going over the same ground. The Holy Spirit needs time to work within everyone's heart and our children need time to digest what's been given them already.

Our three farming or gardening tools should be prayer, words, and actions.

- Prayer softens our children's hearts, so they'll be receptive to God.
- The right words can break through the topsoil of a hardened heart—sowing love, encouragement, and willingness.
- As the farmer must sometimes work hard on tough soil so he can tenderly plant the seed, even so, our actions must at times be tough so we can tenderly plant God's seed.

Before the harvest, however, the farmer will have to deal with the inevitable sprouting thorns and weeds. Killing thorns and weeds without disturbing the newly blooming plants can be hard, tedious work. As teachers, we face the same concerns—nurturing the new plants and killing off the weeds and thorns.

We know that with God's help and wisdom, the planted seeds will eventually grow to fruition.

May God bless your efforts in your garden, and give you a beautiful and abundant harvest this year!

Lord, this gardening is hard work. It takes thought, care, and persistence. Help me to reach the lush growth I see hidden in my children. Give me the patience, foresight, and wisdom to bring about a bountiful harvest. I will do it all for your glory. Amen.

48

Fruit That Lasts

"You did not choose me, but I chose you and appointed you to go and bear fruit—fruit that will last." (John 15:16)

Evangelism and homeschooling have much in common. The ultimate goal of both is bearing fruit that lasts for a lifetime and beyond. Our Scripture theme for the current year is The Great Commission. To help us focus on this theme, the girls and I have been reading *Gentle Persuasion* by Joseph Aldrich. The book provides some great techniques for sharing the gospel, as well as some interesting comparisons between evangelism and homeschooling:

- People want to be seen as individuals.
- Repeated, positive contacts play a key role.

- Fellowship and discipling are musts.
- Fruit bears fruit. [23]

Evangelism isn't effective if the main focus is putting another notch on our belt. Evangelism begins with establishing effective friendships with unbelievers. Then and only then can the door be open to sharing the gospel. In the same way, homeschooling is most effective when we treat our children as individuals. Dealing with each child as a unique individual shows respect for them personally and motivates them to succeed. Listening attentively, answering questions, praising their newest skill, and comforting their hurts are all ways we model Christ to them. Once we've established an intimate and caring relationship with our kids, they'll be much more willing to listen when we speak of Jesus, as well as history, geography, spelling, language, and other subjects.

Studies show that before a person can make an informed, long-lasting decision for Christ, three to five positive contacts with the gospel message are needed. Something as simple as bringing cookies to a new neighbor is one positive contact. Hearing a Christian coworker praise the church is another positive contact. In the same vein, it's important for homeschool moms to repeat instructions and information over and over to our kids. They do their best in a positive environment filled with affirmation and encouragement. So many times I expect my daughters to grasp a concept and put it to use after only one lesson. It doesn't work in evangelism, so why should it in the classroom?

New believers who are welcomed into a church with enthusiastic friendship are more likely to stay long term than those left standing on the sidelines. Along with Christian friendship, they need to be discipled in their new faith—participating in Bible studies, having daily devotions, learning how to share their faith with others, and getting involved in some type of church ministry. Homeschooled children need all these things, too. I encourage my children to love one another, and I constantly tell them how much we love them. If there is one problem I face, it is balancing the role of teacher and disciplinarian. Sometimes I just need to let go and have fun with my children.

Finally, good evangelism sends new converts into the world to share their excitement about the gospel and bring others to Christ. Christians are to be "seed-bearing" people, planting seeds wherever they go. Our goal as homeschool moms is to send our children into the world equipped to plant seeds for Jesus wherever they go. It's the only way to bear fruit from generation to generation.

Dear Lord, make my life count for you. Don't allow the years I've spent educating my children to become fruitless when they graduate. Send them into the world and let them live strong, bold, and courageous lives in your service. Help me nurture the seeds of faith in them now, so that future generations will bear fruit in your name. Amen.

49

Day-to-Day Training

Love the LORD your God with all your heart and with all your soul and with all your strength. These commandments that I give you today are to be upon your hearts. Impress them on your children. Talk about them when you sit at home and when you walk along the road, when you lie down and when you get up. Tie them as symbols on your hands and bind them on your foreheads. Write them on the doorframes of your houses and on your gates. (Deut. 6:5–9)

Spiritual lessons aren't reserved just for Sunday school or our classrooms. We must consistently pass on our faith by breathing in God's Spirit.

Moses gives us many ways to impress God's Word upon our children.

Talking naturally about the Lord within our families is a start. Family devotional time is a good place to share spiritual truths, but this shouldn't be the only time. Any time is the right time, from shopping to sporting events to bedtime; anywhere we are is sharing time with our kids. Seize a particular moment and apply a scriptural truth right then and there. Kids can then equate what just happened with a similar occurrence in the Bible. Relating an appropriate story, Bible verse, or problem from Scripture can make a lasting impression on our children. Jesus himself used this exact technique while speaking to his followers as well as to larger crowds.

Visual expressions are another way in which we can pass on our faith. Jewish men took Moses' instructions literally and began tying phylacteries (small square leather boxes containing Scripture), on their left arms and foreheads during morning prayers. They also placed these leather boxes on the doorpost of their homes to serve as a continual remembrance of God's commandments.

Today's Christians have their own phylacteries. Instead of wearing Scripture, we hang plaques in our homes, put it on bumper stickers, and display it in calendars, books, and pictures all proclaiming God's Word. Several years ago a neighbor of ours remarked about a plaque we have hanging in our home that says:

AS FOR ME AND MY HOUSE, WE WILL SERVE THE LORD (Josh. 24:15).

"I like that *God is boss* sign," he said.

Our neighbor wasn't a Christian, but he certainly understood the message and interpreted it correctly.

Keeping other symbols of God's blessings in view in our home allows us opportunities to present the gospel. We have a "stones of remembrance" bowl containing various rocks, each with a different sticker explaining the blessings it signifies. Every time an unbelieving friend picks up the stones and asks questions about them, we get a chance to share our love for Christ and testify to God's goodness.

Before we can impress God's commandments on our children or others, they must first make an impression on us. This day-to-day training not only passes on the principles of faith, but reaches the teacher as well. Children and unbelievers have a way of noticing when our walk doesn't match our talk. So when they point out our spiritual inconsistencies, it gives us the perfect opportunity to correct ourselves and helps all of us grow spiritually.

Dear Lord, allow your Spirit to permeate our home and our lives today and forevermore. The verses in Deuteronomy challenge me to obey you and impress upon others the importance of obedience to you, too. Help me find unique and interesting ways to reveal you that will excite my kids and spur them on to a life of worship and praise. May they carry the gospel message far beyond the walls of our home and into our hurting and unbelieving world as well. Amen.

50

The Time Is Now

"Sow for yourselves righteousness, reap the fruit of unfailing love, and break up your unplowed ground; for it is time to seek the LORD, until he comes and showers righteousness on you." (Hos. 10:12)

This verse focuses on a different aspect of sowing and reaping—urgency. God is calling for a radical change. He wants his people to become productive and fruitful. He is saying, "Don't put it off, but do it *now!*"

David Starr Jordan said it this way, "Today is your day and mine, the only day we have, the day in which we play our part. What our part may signify in the great whole, we may not understand; but we are here to play it, and now is our time."[24]

Richard Eyre in *Don't Just Do Something, Sit There,* puts it like this:

> It was my maternal grandmother who taught me this one—and taught it, and taught it. "Do it now." "Don't procrastinate." "Get it done."
>
> There were a lot of these shorter variations on the theme, but her favorite was the full-blown and more philosophical-sounding "Never put off until tomorrow what you can do today."[25]

But the new maxim Eyre gives us is: "Always put off a 'put-offable' in favor of a 'now or never.'"[26]

A now-or-never moment might be an opportunity to plant a seed for Christ. Why is it that my children tend to ask deep spiritual questions during the most inopportune times? It's always in the middle of a lesson, at bedtime, or when I'm washing dishes. Sometimes I'm just unwilling to be side-tracked. I hurry right past them and miss what I call "holy moments." But the time is now. I must recognize the opportunities for what they are. I can't put them off!

I know every homeschool mom feels overwhelmed at times—lesson preparation, teaching, housework, bill paying, and on and on. All this stuff needs to be done, but not at the frenetic pace that sometimes happens. God cannot be put off.

As important as the day-to-day necessities are, the time is now when it comes to God and our children.

So what if a sink full of dirty dishes sits unwashed while I devote attention to one of the girls? People are priority, not tasks. It's both urgent and important that we educate our children, but it's not urgent we rush them through the material or force them to finish every task. Skipping the nonessentials gives us freedom to discuss and enjoy our child's question, even if it isn't in the lesson plan. Seeking the Lord now in that holy moment will allow the Lord to shower righteousness on us.

What could be more important than that?

Lord, I am so overwhelmed with all the tasks I have to do. They all seem so urgent. But I'm realizing they're really not, and I'm beginning to see there's only one thing that's urgent: seeking you. As we turn to you, shower us with your righteousness. Amen.

51

Firsthand Experience

Peter and John replied, "Judge for yourselves whether it is right in God's sight to obey you rather than God. For we cannot help speaking about what we have seen and heard." (Acts 4:19, 20)

Peter and John couldn't help but tell others what they'd seen and heard about Jesus. As a believer you can also share your love for Christ within the context of the five senses. It's a terrific way to teach kids about Jesus—explaining how touch, taste, sound, smell, and sight have brought you closer to him.

John described his experiences this way, "That which was from the beginning, which we have *heard*, which we have *seen* with our eyes, which we have *looked at* and our hands have *touched*—this we proclaim concerning the Word of life" (1 John 1:1, *author's emphasis*).

Of course, our experiences with Jesus differ from those of the disciples. We haven't seen him in the flesh, and yet we've seen evidence he lives. People radically change under God's forgiveness. Mountains and canyons, delicate flowers, newborn babies, giraffes and kangaroos all bear the divine stamp. Creation itself is witness to a Creator who's designed everything the eye beholds, and much of it reflects a playful sense of humor at that. A thorough reading of my Bible has completely changed my heart and mind. The truths contained within opened my eyes to reveal God's love in a spectacular way. I need no more convincing!

As a child and even today, I hear God's voice in a gentle rain or a violent thunderstorm, through the whisper of the wind in the trees or the soft lullaby sung by a new mother. Beautiful music sends my soul soaring and sings of a God who delights in harmony and melody. I experience God's presence as I read poetry, devour a book, or participate in a drama.

Our sense of smell might not seem particularly spiritual, but people all over the world use this sublime sense to enhance worship. The tangy odor of incense, the mouthwatering aroma of delicious food, and the delicate scent of a flower all profoundly affect our emotions. God placed such importance on smell that when he gave the Israelites the recipe for temple incense, he told them not to use it for anything but worship. He wanted them to associate that heavenly scent only with him.

Jesus himself introduced worship through taste when he shared bread and wine with his disciples in the very first communion. The Lord truly speaks to me as I share in the Lord's Supper. Even now when I eat an old-fashioned buttermilk donut, I remember the wonderful fellowship Jeff and I had in our first Sunday school class as a married couple.

Touch is a final way in which we can experience God firsthand. Hugs from friends and holding my husband's hand during prayer are some of the most treasured experiences I have. As a young girl I used to sit in church and trace my fingers along the top of my mother's hands; they fascinated me and kept me quiet. Now my daughters do the same thing, and the feeling of closeness it brings me with them is unsurpassed. There is no doubt that God has a part in that feeling.

Have you experienced God through your senses? Ask your children how they've experienced him through sight, sound, smell, taste, and touch. In a myriad of ways he unveils himself to his creation, and in so doing gives each one of us a unique and trustworthy testimony.

Jesus, my Lord, I shouldn't be surprised that you, the Creator of our wonderful human senses, would then use them to win our hearts and draw us ever closer to you. I know there will be even more to experience in heaven, because no eye has seen nor ear heard nor mind conceived what you've prepared for those who love you. I look forward to experiencing you in all your fullness, Lord. You are sense-sational! Amen.

52

Shaking Up the Church

"Now, Lord, consider their threats and enable your ser-
vants to speak your word with great boldness. Stretch out
your hand to heal and perform miraculous signs and
wonders through the name of your holy servant Jesus."

After they prayed, the place where they were meet-
ing was shaken. And they were all filled with the Holy
Spirit and spoke the word of God boldly. (Acts 4:29–31)

Many people question the concept of homeschooling. They wonder why we want to educate
our children this way. Some are concerned that
these kids will be misfits in society by not

179

attending public schools. "What about socialization? Won't they be stymied in making new friends?" they ask. "And what about teacher qualification and certification?"

Early Christian believers, as depicted in the book of Acts, provide an excellent role model for us to follow. When challenged by others, we can look to these faithful men and women, who were also questioned for their faith:

- They told God about the problem.
- They asked him to embolden their witness.
- They asked God to do miracles in Jesus' name.

God honored their prayers, and as a result they turned the world upside down—rumblings that are still being heard today.

If we expect to shake things up in our world, we need to start by telling God about the problem. When people criticize me about homeschooling, my first reaction is to run and complain to someone. I whine to my husband and family. When I was younger, I ran to the adult authority in charge. The believers in Acts went straight to the Lord with their complaints. The Bible shows that every time God's people came to him for help, he responded with his presence, wisdom, and power.

If a person continues to be critical of me and grills me about my faith, I really need to ask for boldness. Yes, I need all the help I can get because boldness is not my strength. But God changes my perspective. He doesn't give me boldness to defend myself or to prove that homeschooling is the only way to educate children. He gives me boldness to witness for Christ. Armed with his power, I am able to face opposition from others with the grace of his Spirit.

Last and most important, I want Jesus to be glorified and even more so in critical, questioning situations. I need boldness to ask God to do something miraculous in the life of my children so God gets the glory. If the critics can see changed lives, changed attitudes, and even positive academic achievements—then I hope some of the negative reactions toward homeschooling will change.

Early Christians responded to criticism and persecution by giving the situation over to God, and he literally shook the building where they were meeting. Then he sent them out into the world filled with the boldness of the Holy Spirit indwelling them.

Just think what God could do today with totally committed believers who are a result of Christian homeschooling.

Lord, I kneel before you, pleading for Holy Spirit boldness to be present in me. Educating these children is pretty tough at times. Thank you for promising to carry me through it all. There will always be some who won't understand why we homeschool or why we choose you above all else. Allow me to respond to them with a graceful, Christ-like spirit and bring all glory to you. Amen.

Endnotes

1. Coralee Elliott Testar, *The Little Kidnappers,* based on "The Kidnappers" by Neil Paterson (Salt Lake City, Utah: Bonneville Worldwide Entertainment Broadcast House, 1990), videocassette.

2. Sam Wellman, *Gladys Aylward: Missionary to China* (Ulrichsville, Ohio: Barbour Publishing, Inc., 1998), 7.

3. Dave and Neta Jackson, *Flight of the Fugitives*: Trailblazer books #13 (Minneapolis, Minnesota: Bethany House Publishers, 1994), back cover.

4. Lloyd Ogilvie, *God's Best for My Life* (Eugene, Oregon: Harvest House Publishers, 1981) July 30.

5. *Martin the Cobbler,* based on Leo Tolstoy's "Where Love Is, There God Is Also," (Racine, Wisconsin: Golden Book Video, 1977, 1987).

6. Dale Hanson Bourke, *Turn Toward the Wind: Embracing Change in Your Life* (Grand Rapids, Michigan: Zondervan Publishing House, 1995), 127.

7. *American Heritage Dictionary* (Boston, Massachusetts: Houghton Mifflin Company, 1982).

8. W.E. Vine, Merrill F. Unger, William White, Jr., *Vine's Complete Expository Dictionary of Old and New Testament Words* (Nashville, Tennessee: Thomas Nelson Publishers, 1985).

9. Frank Alvarez III, *The Annals of a Satanist* (Boise, Idaho: Heavensent, Inc. Publishing, 2001), 174.

10. Charles R. Swindoll, *The Quest for Character: Inspirational Thoughts for Becoming More Like Christ* (Portland, Oregon: Multnomah Press), 146.

11. Jamieson, Fausset, and Brown's *Commentary on the Whole Bible* (Grand Rapids, Michigan: Zondervan Publishing House, 1961), 1003.

12. Beth Sharpton, "When Food Was My Master," *Women Alive*, March/April 1994.

13. Dr. Robert Hemfelt, Dr. Frank Minirth, and Dr. Paul Meier, *We Are Driven: The Compulsive Behaviors America Applauds* (Nashville, Tennessee: Thomas Nelson Publishers, 1991), 217–218.

14. Joanne Shetler with Patricia Purvis, *And the Word Came With Power: How God Met & Changed a People Forever* (Portland, Oregon: Multnomah Press, 1992), 114.

15. "Westminster Shorter Catechism" (1647) (New York: Office of the General Assembly, 1983), 7.007– .010.

16. Charles R. Swindoll, *Rise and Shine: A Wake-Up Call* (Portland, Oregon: Multnomah Press, 1989), 20.

17. Dr. James C. Dobson, *Parenting Isn't For Cowards* (Waco, Texas: Word Books Publishers, 1987), 107.

18. Luci Swindoll, Marilyn Meberg, Patsy Clairmont, Barbara Johnson, *Joy Breaks* (Grand Rapids, Michigan: Zondervan Publishing House, 1997), 79.

19. Leroy Brownlow and Judy Buswell, *Flowers That Never Fade* (Fort Worth, Texas: Brownlow Publishing, 1991).

20. Bob Phillips, *Powerful Thinking for Powerful Living* (Eugene, Oregon: Harvest House Publishers, 1991), 268.

21. Ravi Zacharias and Kevin Johnson, *Jesus Among Other Gods: Youth Edition* (Nashville, Tennessee: Word Publishing, 2000), 5, 39.

22. Ibid., 39.

23. Joseph Aldrich, *Gentle Persuasion*, (Sisters, Oregon: Multnomah Publishers, 1988).

24. Herbert V. Prochnow, *A Funny Thing Happened on the Way to the Podium* (New York: Gramercy Books, 1998), 291.

25. Richard M. Eyre, *Don't Just Do Something, Sit There: New Maxims to Refresh and Enrich Your Life* (New York: Simon and Schuster, 1995), 29.

26. Ibid., 33.